FISHING CANALS

FISHING CANALS

Ken Cope

Foreword by Peter Maskell

DAVID & CHARLES
Newton Abbot   London   North Pomfret (Vt)
In association with ANGLING TIMES

By the same author

The Angling Times Book of the Severn

British Library Cataloguing in Publication Data

Cope, Ken
  Fishing canals.
  1. Fishing – Great Britain
  2. Canals – Great Britain
  I. Title
  799.1'2   SH605
    ISBN 0–7153–7887–2

Library of Congress Catalog Card Number: 79–55994

© EMAP National Publications Ltd 1980

Photoset, Printed in Great Britain
by Redwood Burn Limited, Trowbridge & Esher
for David & Charles (Publishers) Limited
Brunel House   Newton Abbot   Devon

Published in the United States of America
by David & Charles Inc
North Pomfret   Vermont 05053   USA

Contents

Acknowledgements

The author wishes to thank Mr Tom Leatherland, Fisheries Officer, British Waterways Board, and the many anglers and club officials who have willingly supplied up-to-date information on canals throughout the country.

Foreword

Britain's networks of canals, which run like arteries through the body of the country, have been of major significance to the sport of angling for more than a century.

It was the canals running through and linking the industrial heartlands of the nation that the industrial workers of the North and Midlands fished during the last century.

Men who spent their working week cooped up in factories and mines naturally sought out what little fresh air and rural peace they could find on their infrequent rest days. The canals, and the sport of angling, provided a local solution in those areas of limited opportunity.

Much has changed during the last hundred years. Working conditions have become more tolerable. The industrial worker has become more affluent and his leisure opportunities far greater.

The canals themselves have become important leisure centres, with both anglers and pleasure boaters sharing the water. The quality of sport on many of the canals has varied, over the years, from excellent to poor. Pollution from industry is an ever-present threat which can wipe out thriving fish stocks overnight.

Fortunately anglers seem to be succeeding, slowly but surely, in their efforts to keep canals clean enough to support a healthy fish population.

During the last few years the quality of sport has improved on the majority of canals after the mystery fish diseases of the sixties that decimated fish stocks. As a result canal fishing is currently enjoying an unprecedented boom with novice and expert anglers alike lining the towpaths each weekend.

This book contains all the information that any canal angler, either novice or expert, will need to know. It is packed with sound advice and useful tips on how to catch the major species; the best baits to use for each fish and how to prepare those baits; the best tackle and tactics to use and even where to obtain permits to fish all the best stretches of the major canals.

The author, Ken Cope, is a nationally known angling writer who began his angling career on the maze of canals in the Black Country. His knowledge of fishing is extensive and he has fished most of the stretches of the country's canals many times over. The book must surely become the canal angler's bible – an invaluable reference book that will not only help improve his catches but also give him hours of enjoyable reading in the years to come.

PETER MASKELL

1 History of Canals

Canals have a long and fascinating history stemming back to the mid-eighteenth century. The first modern canal, in fact, was partly opened as early as 1757. Named the Sankey Brook (St Helens) it was cut to carry coal from mines in the St Helens area to the River Mersey and up the River Weaver to the salt works in Cheshire. Before this first canal was built, several rivers had been canalised and made navigable to improve transport facilities, so artificial waterways to connect rivers all over the country were a natural progression, especially when we realise that at that time there was almost no other means of moving heavy goods and coal.

Two years after the opening of the Sankey Brook, the young Duke of Bridgewater, then 23 years old, received authorisation through a special Act of Parliament to construct the Bridgewater Canal from Worsley to near Manchester, and soon afterwards had permission to extend it to Manchester and Runcorn. The Duke, who had studied canals on the Continent and who had no doubt noted the success of the Sankey Brook, financed the canal himself.

His consultant was James Brindley, a self-taught engineer with a brilliant mind who later built many more canals. But Brindley's first task, the Bridgewater, was his training ground and he proved his genius in the face of scorn and ridicule by building an aqueduct to take the canal over the River Irwell. The aqueduct was a huge triumph and a wonder of its time, and by 1762 barges were carrying coal across it into Manchester. Later, when the Manchester Ship Canal was built, the aqueduct was replaced by the present Barton Swing Aqueduct.

Brindley next constructed the Trent and Mersey (then called the Grand Trunk because of the number of branches

expected to spring from it) which linked the Bridgewater
Canal to the River Trent. The Staffordshire and Worcester,
which connected the Grand Trunk to the River Severn at
Stourport with a branch at Birmingham, was also engineered
by Brindley. Then he built the Coventry and Oxford Canals
to link the Grand Trunk with the River Thames at Oxford.
The final linking of the rivers Mersey, Trent, Severn and
Thames was not completed however till many years after
Brindley's death in 1772.

The success of the Bridgewater Canal, and the Trent and
Mersey, which was also financed by the Duke of Bridgewater
together with Josiah Wedgwood (founder of the famous
pottery firm), inspired wealthy industrialists, colliery owners
and landowners to invest in further projects. They provided
capital to complete Brindley's canals and began others such
as the Leeds and Liverpool across the Pennines.

Around 1772 there was a great upsurge in canal building
and in two years thirty new canals in various parts of the
country were authorised by Parliament. While the early
canals followed the contour lines and made great sweeps
around the countryside to avoid hills and other obstructions,
engineers now became bolder and cut the shortest routes
possible. With plenty of capital available no obstacle was too
great and canals were taken across valleys, up or through
hills, and across rivers.

Most of the great canal engineering feats of that period can
still be seen today. Among the most impressive are Telford's
two aqueducts at Chirk and Pontcysyllte on the Llangollen
Canal.

At Chirk Telford had to cross the Ceriog valley, so he built
ten 40ft arches, 65ft. high, to carry the aqueduct. Four miles
north came an even more formidable barrier –the River Dee –
in a valley the lowest part of which was 120ft below the
canal's level. Undaunted, Telford first considered a series of
locks but, because of the waste of water, gave up the idea in
favour of another aqueduct. It was a tremendous project that
took eight years to complete. The Pontcysyllte Aqueduct,
which is 1,007ft long and supported by 18 pillars, was opened

in 1805 and is now classed as an ancient monument.

By 1820 the canal system was almost complete. Notable additions to Brindley's waterways were three canals across the Pennines, several developments in Yorkshire and Derbyshire, and a link from the River Trent through Leicester to the Grand Union and London.

Also constructed was an intricate network in and around Birmingham with branches to Stratford and Worcester, a ship canal to improve access to Gloucester from the lower Severn, and a number of canals in the industrial areas of South Wales. Three canals connected the River Thames to the Severn or Bristol Avon and, in Scotland, the Forth and Clyde linked Glasgow to the North and Irish Seas. These canals were of all shapes and sizes, varying in width and depth according to the whims of the financiers and engineers.

The next twenty years, to around 1840, saw improvements and additions such as the Shropshire Union from Nantwich to Wolverhampton. Telford built this as well as re-building the Birmingham system and straightening the Oxford Canal. He also went further afield to construct the Caledonian Canal in Scotland.

By 1850 there were thousands of miles of navigable canals and they played a large part in the Industrial Revolution. Added to the commercial traffic, carrying millions of tons a year of goods of all description, came regular passenger services with special express boats travelling day and night with precedence over other canal transport.

Then came the railways, which more or less spelled the end of the canal boom. They came at a time when the most important canals were so congested that they just couldn't cope with the enormous amount of traffic. Also many canals were perpetually short of water, which meant delays at locks. Add to this the fact that passenger rail travel was an instant success, and so profitable that the railways were able to offer cut rates to commerce, and it is easy to see why the great canal period was over. Although some canal companies fought hard to stave off defeat, the end was inevitable and the decline came quickly. Nevertheless, many canals continued to

carry certain goods in quantity, particularly coal, until World
War II.

Now the majority of boats on canals are pleasure craft and
though we find them a nuisance we, as anglers, should look at
the problem in perspective. After all, canals were constructed
to carry boats, and we are fortunate in that most also provide
reasonable fishing. Without boat traffic canals silt up or
become overgrown with weed, as happened to many prior to
1948 before the waterways were nationalised. The British
Waterways Board, which came into existence in 1962, was in
1968 given extended powers and duties, particularly in rela-
tion to recreation and amenity.

A fisheries officer, Mr Tom Leatherland, was appointed
and his work, begun in 1972, is now bearing fruit. In fact,
thanks to a very liberal re-stocking programme which has
seen hundreds of thousands of fish injected into canals
throughout the country, sport along many waterways is now
as good as it ever was. Mr Leatherland has stocked mainly
with carp, roach and bream, and the carp in particular seem
to be doing very well.

I was present when batches of small bream and carp
around the 1lb mark were placed in the Rushall Canal, near
Walsall. Four years later some of those carp had grown into
double-figure fish; many over 10lb have been landed, and
even more lost, and this story has been repeated all over the
country. True, there are still a few miles of virtually barren
canals around, but often this is the result of poor quality
water, which is beyond BWB's control. Progress is being
made, however, thanks to the efforts of Water Authorities.

A perfect example of this took place on the Staffs–
Worcester Canal near Wolverhampton where new and
modern sewage plant, installed by the Severn–Trent Authority, has brought a tremendous improvement in catches. Previously fishing was poor, or non-existent, for miles each side
of the Barnshurst Sewage Works near Autherley Junction.
Now double-figure hauls of roach, gudgeon, bream, perch
etc., are caught, virtually from the course of the discharged
effluent, and catches elsewhere have greatly increased.

2 Approach to Canal Fishing

Many anglers regard canals as poor substitutes for when no other fishing is available, such as in times of flooding. They rarely visit them except on these occasions and, because they lack the necessary knowledge and experience needed to catch the very shy fish, usually have little to show for their efforts at the end of the day.

But the canal specialists of the Midlands and the North know better. They are aware that, although canals have their limitations, they are also capable of yielding good, sometimes excellent, catches to the angler with the right approach. True, the fish are usually more thinly spread and smaller than those in rivers and lakes, but if tackle is scaled down proportionately, a great deal of satisfaction can be enjoyed on the towpath.

Physically, canals were constructed to a similar pattern, with widths varying from 20 to 50ft, depending on the type of boats they were meant to carry. Apart from ship canals, they were dug out in the form of an inverted triangle, but the passing of time, plus thousands of barges, has resulted in many changes in their original contours, which the angler should always bear in mind. For instance the deepest water may not always be in the middle of the canal, but will depend on the actual line or boat road taken by the original barges. It was not always possible or convenient for them to stay in the middle. Often when approaching a bend they tended to hug and scour out a deeper channel either near the towpath or the far bank.

When this happened the middle silted up and the canal bottom became wedge-shaped, and then of course the large

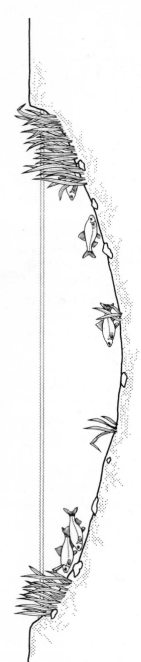

Fig 1 A cross-section of a typical shallow canal. The deepest part is the middle or boat channel, while both shelves slope gently and support plenty of weed growth

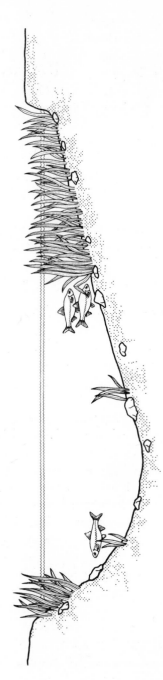

Fig 2 Sometimes the deepest water in the canal is near the far bank, well away from the towpath. This deeper water is often a holding spot for the main shoals, especially in winter

barges ceased plying altogether on most waterways, resulting in the whole of the bed silting up and shallowing. This is why you may often find only three feet of water in the deepest parts.

Although canals are regularly fed and kept topped up by feeder reservoirs, there is normally very little flow except when lock gates are opened, so as far as angling is concerned they are virtually still-water fisheries. There are exceptions, however, and a few, such as the Taunton–Bridgwater, have a perpetual gentle current that calls for certain adjustments to tackle and feeding patterns.

On long exposed lengths, the wind can be a problem as sometimes it pushes the surface water along at a fast rate, which can deceive the inexperienced into thinking that there is an actual flow. But the bottom layers of water will probably be still or even moving gently in the opposite direction.

It is vital for correct bait presentation to find out just what is happening beneath the surface and a good test is to throw in a small piece of lightly mixed groundbait and watch how it sinks. To be on the safe side and to ensure the bait is always presented correctly, the experts fasten their floats by the bottom ring only (peg leg style) and keep the line buried beneath the surface. Of course in very strong winds it may be impossible to hold a float in position, in which case legering tactics are necessary, but generally float methods are superior on narrow waterways.

One of the main problems of the canal angler is finding fish of a particular species. There are few natural holding places where single species can be expected, as in rivers, and in this respect experience along various canals is the only teacher. Knowing the sort of habitats each species prefers is a great help and this is covered later in the book. But generally spots always worth exploring are where small pipes or streams run in. These often carry particles of food that attract the fish.

The areas around overflows or outflows also offer possibilities, as the currents and turbulence again tend to attract fish. Other normally productive spots, especially for bream and tench, are around the basins or arms formerly used for mooring barges. Fish often congregate in these wider areas no doubt feeling more secure, with more space between them and the bank. On the other hand, stretches that should be avoided are where lines of trees or large bushes prevent sunlight falling on the water. The canal bed is usually thick with dead leaves in these heavily shaded lengths, which are almost devoid of fish. Stretches where there is little weed growth are also best left alone.

The main thing to remember when fishing canals is that because the fish are confined in a cramped, still environment, they tend to become very shy and finicky. The slightest activity on the bank is enough to scare them and for this reason it is wise policy to keep well away from the water's edge at all times – even when the water is heavily coloured.

Fish are equipped to sense the smallest vibration. It's part of their defence mechanism. Tackle should always be assembled and laid out quietly. And if there is no cover in the form of high reeds, place the basket or seat (never stand up) as far back from the water as it is possible to get and still be comfortable. If there is not enough room to sit well back it is better to dispense with the basket and sit on a plastic or rubber sheet in order to keep a low profile.

If the water is clear, arm movements, when casting, feeding or playing a fish, should be carried out slowly and smoothly – fast, jerky movements frighten fish – which is why many experts cast underarm or sideways. Terminal tackle should be as fine and hooks as small as conditions allow, though obviously commonsense is needed in this respect as will be seen in the chapters on the various species. These deal with the predominant fish, which are roach, gudgeon, rudd, bream, tench, perch, pike, carp and eels. Chub and dace are sometimes found in canals which are connected to fast-flowing rivers, but they are very thinly spread and hardly worth considering. In any case they can usually be tempted with the falling bait methods described under Roach and Rudd Fishing.

Fortunately for anglers this country is criss-crossed with thousands of miles of canals, especially in the industrial parts

A stretch of the popular Grand Union Canal at Hatton, near Warwick

of the Midlands and the North. Most of these narrow, shallow waterways offer fishing of sorts. Sometimes it is excellent, often it is indifferent, and occasionally it is very poor. But no matter what the quality there are always anglers ready to try their luck along the towpath.

Indeed, as the pressure for space along river banks is increased by an ever-growing army of anglers, more and more are turning to the canals for their sport. The steep increase in the cost of motoring and the high price of bait have also played no small part in encouraging anglers, particularly match fishermen, to spend more time on their local canals. Often in industrial areas these are within easy reach and it is becoming quite common on a summer evening to see them lined with anglers.

Whereas in my part of the world, the West Midlands, anglers formerly headed for the Rivers Severn, Avon or Trent at the slighest opportunity, they now consider the cost of petrol and instead make for the closer 'cuts'. From June 16 to late August there are competitions almost every evening in mid-week, and weekend matches take place all through the season. More often than not the weights at these contests are pitiful and consist of a few ounces. But, as most anglers would agree, any fishing is better than none. They go because they like to be by the waterside, even if the scenery is an eyesore of old oil drums and warehouse walls.

Of course, I am describing now the town lengths that are lined with factories. Out in the country or even the urban districts canals are usually picturesque and tranquil, offering relaxation from the grind of everyday life. Unfortunately, fish stocks in most canals were drastically reduced in the mid 1960s when UDN killing diseases affected many waters throughout the country. Roach, which formed the bulk of canal stocks, were particularly hard hit and virtually wiped out in most waterways.

Now, however, there is evidence that roach and other species are returning in large numbers. Some canals are almost back to those pre-1960 standards, with thriving stocks of fish. The much maligned British Waterways Board is helping in this respect with a long-term re-stocking programme.

Clubs and associations, in conjunction with Water Authority Fisheries Departments are also doing valuable work in cleaning out and maintaining as well as re-stocking long lengths of waterways. The giant Birmingham Anglers' Association, for instance, control hundreds of miles of canal fishing which they are always striving to improve. A major BAA project was a long-term fish survey in conjunction with the former Severn River Authority on the Worcester–Birmingham canal. A lot of valuable information about the habits of canal fish was gathered by groups of anglers and biologists working together over a two-year period.

I attended several of the surveying operations, and it was interesting to note that even when parties of anglers couldn't get so much as a bite between them in four hours' fishing, netting operations carried out immediately afterwards in the same area nearly always revealed quantities of fish. This provided much food for thought and led one of the biologists to remark that canal fishing must be one of the most difficult branches of our sport. I was quick to agree as I have long held the opinion that a good canal angler is a good angler – full stop. He has to be to catch fish from such confined and shallow water. But, if that isn't enough, he has an even bigger problem nowadays and that is the ever increasing boat traffic.

While this is a good thing in one respect – boats help to keep canals from silting up or becoming overgrown with weed – they have a damaging effect on sport. It needs only one boat scraping bottom and stirring up mud and rotting vegetation to spoil the chances of catching fish for hours afterwards.

Match anglers, in big contests, are particularly unfortunate on these occasions. All their hours of preparation and practice go for nothing if a large boat should pass by just before or just after a match has started. I have experienced it and seen it happen so often. Hundreds of anglers frustrated as the water is stirred up into a thick soup-like consistency. Abuse is hurled upon the usually innocent boat owner. He's not to know that there are hundreds of pounds at stake. The abuse is returned, and relations between the two factions become even more strained.

Some progress was made a few years ago in this respect when certain sections of the Oxford Canal were restricted to boats before 11 am on Sundays. It gave contest and pleasure anglers a few hours of undisturbed sport and catches improved enormously.

Canal anglers can make the best of their opportunities by fishing early morning or late evening during the summer, or wait until the boats are laid up in the autumn.

Fishing rights on practically all canals controlled by the British Waterways Board are leased to angling clubs and associations. Individual arrangements vary quite considerably but, as a general rule, the majority of clubs offer facilities to non-members. Apart from possessing the necessary Water Authority's rod licence, all that is usually required is a day ticket which can be obtained on the towpath from patrolling bailiffs as and when fishing takes place.

In addition, certain fisheries are directly controlled by

BWB staff. These are the Shropshire Union Canal (Main Line) and the Llangollen and Middlewich Branches, the Trent and Mersey (Handsacre to Alrewas), the Coventry Canal (Fradley Juntion to Huddlesford Junction) and the Gloucester Canal.

Individual anglers or club secretaries who wish to reserve sections for contests should contact the Amenity Representative at Gloucester or Nantwich as appropriate. The addresses are: Gloucester and Sharpness Canal, Dock Office, Gloucester GL1 2EJ or BWB, Chester Road, Nantwich, Cheshire. Any other information can be obtained from the BWB Fisheries Officer, Willow Grange, Church Road, Watford WD1 3QA.

3 Tackle

Making do with any old rod has led to many stories about the one that got away, which is why successful anglers always carry several different rods no matter where they go. This is no trouble these days as modern hollow fibre glass and carbon fibre models, besides being strong and virtually unbreakable, are extremely light.

Rods for floatfishing, legering, piking, carping, plus perhaps a roach pole for the odd tiddler-snatching session, can be stowed in a hold-all and carried for long distances with little effort. Of course, those who specialise in one particular branch of angling, such as matchmen, can limit their choice. But often even the specialist finds himself in a situation where he wishes he had brought a certain rod with him, which is why it always pays to be prepared.

The all-round canal angler is no exception and, though his field in regard to varying types of water is limited, he still requires a selection of rods if he is to make the most of his opportunities.

Floatfishing rods
Although most canals are quite narrow it pays to use a fairly long rod (at least 12 foot) for floatfishing. A rod of this length allows you to sit well back from the water's edge on clear canals, and also helps towards achieving the delicate float control required on hard-fished waters. Hollow fibre-glass tip-actioned match rods, which are extremely light yet quite powerful, will handle comfortably most species encountered.

For bigger fish, such as tench or bream, which tend to inhabit weedy stretches and for which stronger line is necessary, a stouter general purpose rod is a better proposition as more pressure can be applied if a fish does gain the shelter of weed.

Leger rod

An eight or nine foot light leger rod with a threaded end ring to take a quiver or swing tip is useful for rough conditions on a narrow canal and almost essential for the deeper and wider waterways. To save on expenditure the same rod with a slightly stouter top piece can be used for spinning or eel fishing.

Mini leger rod

A mini-leger rod, as used by many match anglers, is a boon in some situations such as for anchoring a bait in the near margin. They are about six foot long and, together with a small swing or quiver tip, ideal for very close-range fishing in windy weather.

Spinning rod

Great sport can be had spinning for perch and small pike along canals and a light six or seven foot spinning rod, together with a fixed spool reel ensures maximum enjoyment when a fish is hooked. But if there are any big pike around, say over 10lb, it would be wiser to use something more powerful. A stout spinning rod can also be used for live or deadbaiting for pike or eels.

Carp rod

Double figure carp frequent a few canals, but they are extremely difficult to catch in open water and more often than not will take a bait only in very weedy swims. For this kind of fishing where no quarter can be given lest the fish gain the shelter of the weed a very powerful rod is necessary. But for smaller carp in fairly open waters a general purpose 12-footer is quite adequate.

Roach poles

Hollow fibre-glass or, if you can afford them, carbon-fibre roach poles in varying lengths from nine to 20 foot are very popular among match anglers for canal fishing. This is because the reel can be dispensed with, thus speeding up operations. Also, a long pole can be a boon in windy weather (providing it is not so windy as to make holding it difficult) as you can fish with the tip right over the float, thus preventing line drag.

There are two kinds of pole, the take-apart in which the sections (usually five or six) are separate, and the telescopic. The take-apart models are the most popular as they can be easily lengthened or shortened while actually playing a fish – a great advantage when a big one is hooked. Lines and tackles for pole fishing are made up beforehand and measured so that fish swing comfortably to hand. They are carried on line wrappers and fastened to the end of the pole by two or three short lengths of rubber tubing.

Reels

A fixed spool reel with several spools carrying lines of various breaking strains is adequate for all methods of canal fishing. Whether you prefer a closed or open faced model is a personal choice, as there is little to choose between them. However, the closed face models have an advantage in windy weather in that there are no loops of line hanging loose to become tangled.

No matter what your choice always ensure the clutch is set or adjusted to slip when extra strong pressure is applied, as this can prevent many tackle smashes when a big fish is hooked unexpectedly. Many anglers, of course, dispense with the slipping clutch, preferring to allow the reel to wind backwards when a fish puts on pressure.

Because long casting is unnecessary, a lot of canal anglers use a centre pin reel, their argument being that it is less complicated to use and less likely to cause tangles. They have a point too, especially in windy weather or when overhanging trees and bushes make casting difficult. Certainly centre pins are handier for close range work – and remember many fish are hooked virtually under the rod tip. Here I think it worth mentioning that one of the country's top canal match anglers, Bill Makin from Hinckley, Leicestershire, invariably uses a centre pin reel. Bill has landed carp up to 9lb on a size 20

hook tied to 1lb breaking strain line with a centre pin – a feat
he reckons he might not have achieved with a fixed spool.

Bill's argument is that with his centre pin he feels more in
contact with a hooked fish. He controls the reel with fingers
resting lightly on the rim and reckons he can more or less
judge what his quarry will do next by the pressure on the line.

The all-round canal angler requires several spare spools for
his reel, each filled with line of different strength and some
duplicated in case of accidents such as 'birds nests', etc. Line
strength to use will obviously vary according to what species
are the quarry but an average selection would be 1½lb breaking strain for match fishing or tiddler snatching, 2½ to 3lb
b.s. for tench, bream and light spinning for perch, and 5lb or
6lb b.s. for small pike, carp or eels. However, if really big pike
or carp are the target (i.e. double figure fish) lines of up to
12lb b.s. would not be out of place in some circumstances.

There are dozens of different brands of line on the market
and, by and large, there is little to choose in the more expensive range. Choice, therefore, is more or less personal preference. Points to look for are suppleness (the cheaper brands
are often too springy, which causes 'birds nests'), elasticity,
colour and diameter-strength ratio. I mention the latter
quality because some brands tend to be thicker for the same
breaking strain than others. In most circumstances the
smaller the line diameter the easier it is to handle.

Colour of the line again comes down to personal preference.
I have always favoured a sorrel shade, especially for the hook
lengths. Some brands are now advertised as being of a colour
that is invisible in water which, if true, is obviously the ultimate, as nothing could be better. A tip here: always test new
line in numerous places as it is being wound on to the reel
spool.

Monofilament sometimes deteriorates, especially if it has
been subjected to sunlight and it may have lain in the tackle
dealer's window. I learned this lesson the hard way when
some supposedly 3lb b.s. line kept snapping like cotton just
when I had a shoal of good bream feeding. After losing four
sliding float rigs in succession as I struck into big fish, I

checked the rest of the line on the spool and, even though I had purchased it only the previous day it was virtually rotten.

Finally on the subject of lines I would remind you to always fill or load the reel spool to within $\frac{1}{16}$in of the lip and you will find your casting much smoother. The easy way to do this is to wind a hundred yards of a particular breaking strain on to the spool and then fill the rest of the spool with backing material – wool and nylon, or even PVC tape. Now reverse the process and you will never have any trouble with replacement 100 yard lengths.

Hooks

Apart from contest work no special hooks are necessary for canal fishing. Spade ends are the most popular these days though many carp and eel specialists maintain that the straight, eyed variety are more reliable with stout line. But whatever your choice it pays to buy hooks in bulk and tie your own to whatever brand and strength of line you prefer.

Tying spade end hooks is simplicity with practice but for those whose fingers are not up to the job hooktying devices which work extremely well are on the market. Of the many different patterns of hooks available I suppose long and medium shanked crystal and round bends are the most popular and reliable. But again, it comes down to what you like best. For instance, I have little faith in short shanked hooks and always have difficulty extracting them from the fish, yet many anglers swear by them.

Canal match anglers are very hook conscious, as they have to be. They invariably plump for fine wire patterns in sizes from 16 to 24. The all-rounder, however, carries a much wider selection from perhaps size 4 upwards and including a few trebles for pike and eel fishing.

The colour of the hook can be important, particularly in clear-water canals, but there are many arguments on the subject. Some anglers swear by gilt hooks while others are equally adamant that bronze, black or blued are a more natural colour. The only solution to this question is to make your own choice by experimenting while the fish are feeding.

In the past I have gone so far as to paint white the shanks of black hooks for hempseed fishing, the idea being that the white shank would emphasise the white 'sprout' or 'shoot' of the black seed, making it more attractive. However, my experiment made little difference to my catches so I finally came to the conclusion that it was a waste of time. I must admit to having great faith in gilt hooks for many baits, because I have, on several occasions, hooked roach with a bare gilt hook, usually while adjusting my tackle for depth. These experiences have led me to believe that gilt hooks can enhance the attractiveness of maggots.

Floats
The prime functions of a float are to help carry and present a bait to the fish in as natural a manner as possible and to signal bites clearly. This is often easier said than done, however, and there are dozens of different types on the market designed to overcome problems such as very deep or shallow water, fast currents, great widths, etc. Fortunately, the canal angler has little to worry him in this respect and he can limit his range to three or four patterns that will cope with most conditions he is likely to encounter. Except in the very wide canals long casting is rarely called for, currents, if any, are gentle and depths rarely exceed five or six feet. But the wind is frequently troublesome and is often the greatest influence on the final choice of float.

Because very little weight is required to get the bait down to the fish many anglers 'load' their canal floats by wrapping lead wire around the base until just one, sometimes two, small shots are needed to cock them, so making them extremely sensitive. But less sensitive, slightly bulkier floats are required on occasions such as for perch or tench fishing with lobworms, or when seeking large roach or bream with breadflake.

A problem frequently encountered on canals, particularly when fishing the far side, is spotting the float among the

An angler swings on a small roach to hand during an open match on a recognisably hot summer day various shadows cast by overhanging reeds and bankside vegetation. For this reason it is wise to carry sets of the same floats, each with a different coloured tip. Light green or yellow are favourite colours for far bank fishing, while the more popular orange, red and black are easily seen when fishing the middle or close in.

Quills of all types make excellent canal floats for many different styles of fishing. Because they are extremely buoyant they are particularly useful for the larger baits such as lobworms, yet they are sensitive enough when correctly trimmed to signal the faintest bites.

Quills come into their own in rough, windy weather when a little extra weight is required to prevent the bait being dragged unnaturally along the bottom. The crow quill, with its buoyant tip and long stem, is a great favourite, as is the porcupine – the heaviest of the quill floats. Peacock quills have an extra advantage in that they can be easily cut into different sizes to serve varying purposes. Small stick floats are ideal for presenting small baits close in and over the far side of a canal in calm windless conditions.

Made from heavy cane stems with slim balsa bodies, 'sticks' provide plenty of weight to help casting, and they need very little lead shot to trim them down to a mere pimple on the surface. They are very sensitive and particularly useful for 'laying on' across the canal with casters or maggots.

Small antenna floats made from a cane stem and balsa body, which are often loaded to aid casting, are a firm favourite among canal match anglers. In fact they rarely use any other type. There are several different designs on the market but they all have one thing in common – a very slender tip that disappears below the surface the moment a fish takes the bait. Obviously, this type of float is only suitable for small baits in reasonable weather conditions. For rough weather or for bigger and heavier baits a similar design but with a thicker tip is necessary.

For the wider and deeper canals such as the Gloucester, where the depth can be as much as 14ft, wagglers and small sliding floats carrying a fair amount of weight are needed to aid casting and to get baits down quickly. Bodied wagglers, carrying the equivalent of 2½ swan shot are regularly used by the Gloucester Canal experts. They weight them until only the merest 'pimple' is visible on the surface and, trimmed this way wagglers, despite their bulk, can be extremely sensitive.

My own favourite Gloucester Canal float is a smallish cane and balsa slider based on a pattern designed by former world champion Billy Lane especially for the 1963 National Championship on that water.

Carrying the equivalent of 3 AAA or one and a half swan shot, my small sliders can also be used as wagglers, and they are a joy to use. While I must admit that the sliding float method is somewhat old fashioned in these days of intensive legering, it's a technique that gives me great pleasure and I still use it as often as possible on the Gloucester 'cut'. I find it particularly effective for registering 'drop' and 'lift' bites as, when shotted correctly, the long, slim cane stem rises like a periscope at the slightest nibble.

Small Continental floats, with a thin nylon bristle tip, are becoming popular among canal match anglers, but they are so sensitive – one or two micro dust shot are often enough to trim them down to the tip – that they need to be set up and shotted at home. Match anglers carry these ultra-sensitive tackles on special line winders and use them mainly in conjunction with a roach pole.

Accessories

Umbrella Attachment
It is often impossible to force an umbrella pole into the hard tow path along many canals. The answer is some kind of attachment fastened to one side or the back of the seat box or basket into which the umbrella pole can be inserted and clamped. If you haven't got such an attachment and are caught in a heavy downpour, a useful tip is to insert the pole inside the collar and down the back of your coat holding it tight with the belt. It's a bit uncomfortable but it enables you to carry on fishing without getting wet.

Throwing Sticks and Catapults

These are a must for accurate loose feeding any bait across the far side, especially in windy weather. Personally I prefer a stick for narrow waterways as, besides being less trouble to load and use, the stick holds the bait together in a tighter group than a catapult. My home-made one – I fashioned it from an old cane rod butt – enables me to place a pinch of squatts or groundbait or half a dozen casters right under the far bank with little effort even while sitting.

Bread Punch

Invented by those renowned canal anglers from Lancashire, the bread punch is placed high on my list of canal tackle. Designed mainly to attract small roach, it also works equally well for sizeable fish, especially in winter. There are many types of punch available on the market but the most popular is one that has four interchangeable screw-in heads which produce different sized bread pellets ranging from $\frac{1}{16}$in to $\frac{1}{4}$in diameter.

Swing and Quiver Tips

Although swing and quiver tips are normally associated with wide flowing rivers and lakes, smaller versions are very effective for canal fishing in rough conditions.

Weed Drag

Weed is often a problem, especially in disused and abandoned canals, but it can be removed easily with a drag made from two garden rake heads bound or welded together. The drag is also useful for raking a swim prior to tench fishing – a ploy that often induces tench to feed.

Lead Shot

As well as the normal range of shot, the Continental leads (known as 'mouse droppings') and olivettes are used by some canal anglers, particularly for pole fishing. Personally I find Continental leads more difficult to remove and adjust than our own soft lead shot so I never bother with them. A coil of lead wire is a useful addition to the shot box as it can be used for loading the base of floats for those occasions when fish are feeding in mid water or on the surface, so calling for a slow sinking bait. A short length of lead wire squeezed on the line in an 'S' shape is a must for hempseed fishing because ordinary shot are often mistakenly grabbed by the fish, giving false bites.

Swimfeeders

These, at least the mini type, have been used successfully on the Gloucester Canal and I have no doubt that they will eventually catch on along other wide and deep canals. But whether they will ever become popular along the narrow 'cuts' is doubtful – it would be like using a sledgehammer to crack a nut.

Nevertheless, many anglers, particularly in the West Midlands, use the gadget wherever they go so I shan't be surprised to see them along the tow paths.

Other useful items of tackle are: a pair of artery forceps for extracting large or treble hooks, swivels and wire traces for pike fishing, plus a bait kettle for carrying livebaits.

4 Baits

Bloodworms and Jokers

The bloodworm is a natural food for most fish and is therefore a deadly bait, particularly in canals, which are ideal breeding grounds for these worms. The Bridgewater Canal, in Lancashire, is reputed to be alive with them in certain areas.

Larvae of the midge, bloodworms have one disadvantage in that they attract mostly small fish and are therefore used mainly by match anglers. Not that bloodworms won't attract better samples; they will, as I once saw demonstrated by Belgian match champion Pierre Michiels at Coombe Lake, near Coventry. Fishing in an invitation contest along with scores of English stars, Pierre used bloodworms to devastating effect, catching big roach, and bream to 4lb (along with the usual tiddlers) for a total weight in excess of 17lb. He didn't win the match but his methods convinced me of the importance of bloodworms as a bait in this country.

Lancashire anglers, of course, need no convincing, for these small worms have been the number one bait in Northern canal contests for a hundred years or more – when the rules have allowed. Because of its deadly attraction, plus the fact that it is not too easy to obtain, bloodworm has always been considered an unfair advantage and consequently banned in certain parts of the country. But where it is permitted, the bloodworm experts are never far from the top of the prize lists and, if the fishing is poor, they invariably come out winners. That is the main advantage of this bait; it attracts fish when everything else has failed. I know I have said this about certain types of maggots, but bloodworm really is the ultimate attractor.

Since the ban on its use was lifted by the NFA, and consequently many angling associations, bloodworm has become a first-choice bait with a great number of canal matchmen. Its advocates are not always successful, but it's a safe bet that if sport is slow they are usually at the top of the prize lists.

Because of the demand by match anglers, bloodworm can now be obtained at most tackle shops to order. But it can be expensive, especially during the winter months when the demand tends to exceed the supply. Most bloodworm is gathered in Lancashire where, for some strange reason, the larvae seems to thrive to a much greater extent than in the rest of the country. Or is it that the Lancashire lads, with their much longer experience, are more skilled in finding the worms?

Bloodworm can be found in most still or sluggish water but not always in great quantity. The richest supplies seem to come from shallow ponds or canals with muddy bottoms. Several men in Lancashire make a good living by collecting and selling the bait. They gather the worms, which are about an inch long and ¹⁄₁₆in in width, with a special tool which consists of a flat blade of zinc or aluminium, or any pliable metal that doesn't rust, fastened to the end of a long pole. The blade, which is about two inches wide, 18in long and ¹⁄₁₆in thick, is attached to the pole (which could be a broom handle) in such a way that when the handle is vertical the flat blade is parallel to the ground.

In use, the blade is scraped slowly across and just beneath the surface of the mud and the bloodworms are caught up on the front edge of the blade. The action is similar to scything grass in that the blade is swept down and across the surface of the mud and up through the water in one slow smooth stroke. This movement washes the mud from the blade as it rises to the surface yet holds the bloodworms on the front edge.

The worms are now scraped off the blade and put in a container ready for cleaning. In winter the worms bury themselves in the mud, so it is necessary to sink the blade deeper before starting to scrape. Cleaning the bloodworms and removing excess mud is done with a fine mesh cloth. A lady's nylon stocking is ideal for this purpose. Simply cut off the foot, tie a knot in the top, and tip the bloodworms into it. Now dip the stocking into the water and carefully knead out as much mud as possible, or if preferred take it home and wash away the mud under the cold water tap.

One advantage with the stocking is that surplus water can be easily got rid of by swinging it round in the air as we do with keepnets. When reasonably dry tip the bloodworms on to a sheet of newspaper and remove any remaining rubbish. The final drying and separating of the worms is best done with black peat which should be sprinkled over them immediately. When they are separated fold the newspaper to prevent them escaping and then wrap them in a second sheet to make doubly sure and store them in a fridge set several degrees above freezing. Don't store them for too long though as they die after about a week in summer and two weeks in winter.

Jokers are very similar to bloodworms but much smaller and livelier. So lively in fact that their antics in the water awaken and attract the most lethargic fish, which is why they make such excellent feeders. Jokers and bloodworms work in the same way as squatts and pinkies; in other words the small jokers, or squatts, get the fish interested and pre-occupied with a certain kind of food so that they are immediately attracted to a slightly larger morsel of the same type – the bloodworm or the pinkie.

Larvae of the gnat, jokers hatch out in the same way as bloodworms except that they are always found in running shallow streams. You never find them in clear water. They are gathered, cleaned and stored in exactly the same manner as bloodworms but, because they are smaller, many more are required.

While match anglers reckon to need say, two or three hundred bloodworms for a three-hour contest, they would need half a pint, or thousands, of jokers. Again, like bloodworms, jokers can be purchased to order these days, but they are even more difficult to get hold of in the winter.

Breadcrust

Breadcrust is a good canal bait used mainly by carp specialists, but it will also tempt roach and rudd. One of its main

advantages is its extreme buoyancy, which makes it ideal for
surface or mid-water fishing on hot summer days. But it also
attracts fish on the bottom and, because it sinks very slowly,
often proves the only answer to the more weedy swims. In
fact, when the bottom of a canal is covered in blanket-weed –
a common occurence along disused waterways – breadcrust
comes into its own as it is probably the only bait that won't
sink in the weed out of sight.

The big disadvantage with breadcrust is that it crumbles
very easily when soaked and tends to fall off the hook at the
slightest disturbance. The only way to overcome this is to use
a larger hook than usual and pass it through the crust two or
three times, finally burying the point as near the crust as possible. Although some anglers prepare breadcrust overnight by
dampening and pressing it, this is not really necessary for
canal fishing.

Breadflake

Breadflake is a fine bait for all bottom and surface feeding
fish, and even pike are not averse to grabbing a piece occasionally. It is most effective in clear water during the summer
but it is also good in winter, and many canal anglers prefer it
to all other baits.

Flake can be offered in small or large pieces depending on
what you are hoping to catch but, generally speaking, it pays
to start with small portions and scale up if you feel there are
bigger fish in the swim.

Whether you use large or small pieces, it is important to
ensure the bread is really fresh, otherwise it won't stay on the
hook. Sliced, steam-baked loaves are ideal as this type of
bread is moist and clings well. The flake is best fastened to the
hook by folding it around the shank and gently squeezing it
together. This leaves the point of the hook clear for easy penetration on the strike.

Bread Paste

On its day bread paste is one of the most deadly canal baits
for roach, bream and several other species. It is good in

summer and excellent in winter, yet like many other traditional baits, it has fallen out of fashion and is rarely used these
days except by a few old timers.

Years ago match anglers in certain parts of the country
rarely bothered with any other bait than bread paste which is
surely a testimony as to its effectiveness. Stafford anglers in
particular achieved a formidable reputation as 'paste' experts
and offered tough opposition along the Trent and Mersey and
Staffs–Worcester Canals. Although the fish they caught were
mainly tiny roach, they often hooked big fish of other species
such as bream and tench, again proving the bait's attractiveness.

As an example, I remember when George Parr, from
Rugeley near Stafford, once netted over 9lb of quality and
small roach in a three-hour contest on the Trent and Mersey
at King's Bromley. This catch was exceptional even for the
late 1950s when the canal, in the Lichfield area, was at its
best, and is a record match weight that, to the best of my
knowledge, still stands.

The Stafford 'paste men', as they were known, designed a
special float to help present the bait more precisely and deli-
cately. A large antenna-bodied type, it had a heavily loaded
base and was a forerunner of the well known zoomer pattern.

Armed with these floats, which needed only a flick of the
rod tip to send them to the far side of the canal, and a knob of
very soft bread paste stuck on the rod butt just above the
centre pin reel, the paste specialists proved difficult to beat.

One of their secrets was in the mixing of the paste. All sorts
of ingredients were added to make it more attractive.
Generally however, the main essential was to mix the paste to
as soft a consistency as possible so that it would just, and only
just, cling to the hook long enough to tempt a fish.

To attach the bait they simply pulled the hook through the
knob of paste on the rod butt or smeared it on between finger
and thumb. Although only the merest fragment of paste clung
to the hook it was enough to do the job.

The invention of the bread punch, plus the caster revolution, coupled with the fish diseases in the mid sixties, spelled

the end of paste fishing, but it is a method that could easily be revived. It needs only one angler to achieve some success with any bait to start a chain reaction, as we have seen with the way that bronze maggots have ousted casters on most waters. I certainly wouldn't be surprised to see paste fishing come back, particularly in winter when the canals are clear.

Mixing paste to the correct consistency calls for some experience in its use. A main requirement is stale bread: new loaves are best kept for fishing flake. Hard bread, say at least a week old, is ideal as it mixes very smoothly and without lumps. One of the simplest ways of making paste is to cut away the crust from two or three rounds of bread, put it into a piece of fine linen cloth, bundle it into a ball and immerse it in cold water. When the bread is soggy, the cloth is twisted to remove as much water as possible. The bread should then be kneaded through the cloth until it is soft and tacky enough to just stay on the hook.

A small quantity of sugar – one teaspoonful to a round of bread – is reputed to give added tackiness but it is not essential. Another way to mix paste is to put the bread in a dish and add boiling water. After it has cooled mix with a fork until it is sloppy and then add finely ground breadcrumb or biscuit meal until you have the correct consistency.

Yellow bread paste – a popular colour for some canals – is made by adding custard powder, turmeric or a dye such as auromine O, to the mixture as it is being kneaded. How the paste is fastened to the hook is not important. What is essential is that the bait should be soft enough to remain on the hook only as long as the tackle is undisturbed. Obviously, the quality of the fish you are after will determine the hook size and the amount of paste used, but don't worry about hiding the hook. As I mentioned earlier the 'paste experts' used a mere smear on the shank of a size 20 or 18 hook and often attracted big fish.

Casters

The caster, or maggot chrysalis to give it its proper name, is without doubt the most widely used bait on all waters in the

British Isles and is only rivalled in popularity by the bronze maggot. It would be true to say that it is a bait that will catch all species of fish from all types of water. Yet, significantly, caster fishing was first evolved on hard-fished canals and the man who led the way is that legendary Lancashire expert Benny Ashurst.

It was in the mid 1950s that Benny and his friends first discovered the potential of casters for catching shy roach from north western canals. Soon they developed a method of offering the bait right across the far side with a new type of float made from balsa and cane (the forerunner of the stick float) and proceeded to clean up at most matches they attended. They also broke many canal match catch records with unheard of weights (often in the teens of pounds) for that period.

Flushed with their success on canals, Benny and the Leigh lads began to visit other waters, notably the River Trent, and again their new bait proved unbeatable, so much so that it was quickly adopted by other anglers, both match and pleasure, who used it to good effect on all kinds of water all over the country. While, at the time of writing, the caster has lost its edge to the bronze maggot on many waters, it is still a number one canal bait that catches fish in all conditions.

Normally casters are used for 'bottom' fishing and any 'floaters' (that is those that won't sink) are discarded. But floaters make an excellent surface bait on canals in summer, as is explained elsewhere.

Although all tackle shops sell casters to order, so few are needed for a successful day's canal fishing (a pint is ample) that it is a simple process to ensure your own regular small supply. All that is required is a ³⁄₁₆in mesh riddle and a little spare time, plus some fully fed maggots. Maggots that have been taken off feed before time will turn into chrysalis eventually, but they are unreliable.

To prepare, place a couple of pints of neat, top quality, uncoloured maggots in a large shallow bowl containing fine, damp sawdust and leave them undisturbed in a warm room. In summer maggots turn naturally within three or four days of leaving the feed but artificial heat is necessary to keep them moving in winter. Judging the timing of the change from lively maggots to first a white soft-cased chrysalis, then orange brown, to reddish brown (which is the latest stage when they will still sink) comes only with experience. For instance, I have known lively maggots turn into dark brown 'floaters' in less than an hour on a hot summer's day.

Tackle dealers, who prepare casters by the gallon and who stand to lose a lot of money if they misjudge their timing, often have to stay up all night in summer to ensure they catch them right. Anyway, inspect the maggots regularly each day until they begin to turn. Top quality, fully fed maggots will begin to change more or less at the same time. When this happens, tip them on to the riddle, which should be suspended over a suitable container. I use a wooden cake tray.

Maggots that haven't turned will crawl through the mesh, leaving the casters behind. Place these in a polythene bag which should be sealed to prevent any air entering. The casters are alive and will survive in the air-sealed bag.

Left in warm surroundings they will continue to turn and eventually float, so place the bag in a refrigerator set at about 35°F. This virtually halts the metamorphosis but not completely, so don't store them for more than a fortnight otherwise you will find you have a bag full of floaters. Repeat the process with the remaining maggots at regular intervals until they have all turned or until you have enough casters.

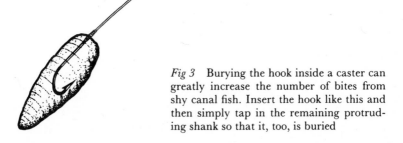

Fig 3 Burying the hook inside a caster can greatly increase the number of bites from shy canal fish. Insert the hook like this and then simply tap in the remaining protruding shank so that it, too, is buried

If you haven't a refrigerator, or if your wife objects to your
storing bait, the casters can be kept safely in water for a few
days. The trouble with this method is that it kills the casters
and they will turn sour, giving off a dreadful smell, so change
the water regularly. Whether or not fish object to sour casters
however is a bone of contention. The majority of anglers
maintain that they do and always use fresh bait. On the other
hand, I know a prominent match angler who thinks the
opposite. He has won many contests, admittedly not on
canals, with months old casters that stank to high heaven.

One of the advantages of casters is that fairly large hooks,
that is in comparison to those used for maggots, can be buried
and completely hidden inside – a boon on hard-fished waters.

Cheese

Cheese is a good traditional bait that has accounted for large
numbers of quality canal roach, not to mention a few other
species. Many a two-pound redfin has fallen for a knob of
Edam, and I know several old-timers who rarely use any
other bait. The big snag with cheese though, is that it tends to
harden when immersed in water, so the softer brands are
always the best.

Edam is a firm favourite with many anglers but others
plump for the processed varieties. Cheese can also be made
into a paste by mixing a few breadcrumbs or a little cornflour
with a slice of a processed variety. If you prefer paste,
however, ensure it is soft enough to allow the hook easy
penetration on the strike or, better still, mould it round the
shank, leaving the point clear. Ordinary cheese should be
lightly hooked with the point passed carefully out through the
side. As with all other baits a few samples should be thrown
into the swim as an attractor, and grated cheese works fine for
this.

Groundbait

In what I consider the golden period of canal fishing, the
1950s and early '60s, we used a large quantity of cereal
groundbait for all species and caught lots of fish. Finely
ground breadcrumbs, sausage rusk or biscuit meal were the

standard ingredients and we mixed them very lightly so that a small, walnut-sized, piece formed a cloud after breaking up on impact with the water.

These days, groundbait is no longer considered indispensable and most anglers, including myself, prefer to loose feed samples of the hookbait whenever possible. Nevertheless, it is a fact that, if used sparingly and intelligently, groundbait will attract and induce canal fish to feed, particularly roach, bream and gudgeon.

Bearing in mind the nature of the water, often shallow and with little flow, the groundbait should be mixed as lightly as possible and used in small pieces, so avoiding too much disturbance when it hits the water. Cloud groundbait, that is non-feeding mixture so fine and lightly mixed that it breaks up and forms a slow-sinking cloud of fine particles, is favoured by most canal anglers when the water is clear.

There is no doubt that cloud groundbait is very effective for small to medium sized fish, especially when a few hookbaits are mixed with it. Fine-texture sausage rusk or biscuit meal forms the best cloud but it should be mixed very carefully and dampened only enough to hold together when lightly squeezed.

If milk is used as a dampener instead of water, the cloud effect is even more pronounced. Malt-dust groundbait was once a great favourite with South Staffordshire canal anglers and, though it is now very rarely used, I feel it merits inclusion as a wonderful non-feeding attractor. Malt, or 'kiln' dust, as it is called in the brewing trade, is a waste product that remains after the malting process. It looks like and has the same texture and colour as cigarette tobacco, but with an attractive malty smell. The only commercial use of malt dust that I am aware of is the making of cattle cake, so it is not too difficult to obtain providing you can find a malting house.

To make groundbait place a couple of handfuls of the dust in a bowl and scald it thoroughly until it is quite sloppy. When cool drain away the surplus dark brown liquid and add two or three cupfuls of biscuit meal or fine breadcrumbs to the remaining malt dust. Rub the mixture between the hands thoroughly, until it is just damp enough to hold together with a spongy feeling when squeezed, and it's ready. For a faster-sinking mixture simply add less cereal or more water.

A very effective canal groundbait for use when fishing with various types of bread baits on the hook, is a sloppy mixture of fine breadcrumbs or biscuit meal. To make it simply add water until it has the consistency of 'runny porridge'. This mixture, which can be flicked into the canal with a spoon, forms a nice cloud as it sinks.

A well known Lancashire canal groundbait is 'Black Magic'. It is mainly used by match anglers when bloodworm fishing. Made from black leaf mould, its effectiveness was discovered during the second world war when, because cereals were banned as groundbait, all kinds of substitutes were tried. Nowadays black lawn peat, as sold in gardening shops, has largely replaced the original substance. It is mixed in the same form as cloud bait – that is only slightly dampened so that it breaks up into a black cloud in the water. Lawn peat is also a good material in which to store bloodworms and 'jokers' and is widely used for this purpose.

Hempseed

My earliest fishing memories are associated with hempseed, an excellent bait for roach and rudd which is particularly effective in clear canals. I can remember vividly the misty, early summer mornings when, as a boy of eight or nine years, I helped my cousin and uncle prepare the 'magic seed' for an outing on the local 'cut'. 'Tell me when the white shoots start to appear', my uncle would say, and my cousin and I would stand glued to the stove, slyly turning up the gas occasionally, impatiently waiting for the seeds to burst as they slowly cooked. Looking back I don't think we ever took any other bait with us. I always had implicit faith that we would catch fish with hemp and we usually did.

In later years I can recall visits to another canal (now alas dried up) when shoals of good sample roach 'boiled' towards the surface whenever I threw in a few hempseeds. In fact, these particular fish became so preoccupied with hemp that merely going through the motions – a wave of the hand – was sufficient to excite them. They behaved like chickens coming to the corn tin.

Unfortunately, round about this time (the early 1950s) hempseed acquired the reputation of being harmful to the fish and fisheries. The seed was said to drug fish to such an extent that they refused to accept any other bait. Other objections were based on an assumption that any seeds not eaten by the fish grew into plants despite being boiled!

It was also thought that excessive use of the bait polluted the water: the only objection I happen to agree with. We now know, of course, that hempseed is a fine fish food but despite this it is still banned on some club waters. What I like about hempseed is that it tends to attract good sample fish as well as tiddlers. In fact, many specimen roach have been taken on a single grain.

Obtainable at most tackle shops and corn merchants, hempseed is of little use in its raw state and must either be soaked for a long period or boiled until the seeds split open to reveal the soft white kernel and small sprout or shoot. For best results the bait should be used sparingly as the seed is full of protein and fish soon get their fill. Half a pint is ample for a day on a canal and any left over after a session should be left on the towpath to feed the birds rather than thrown into the water to go sour.

The quickest way to prepare hempseed is to boil it, but before doing so give the seeds a thorough wash in a sieve held under the cold water tap. Now place them in a saucepan, add plenty of water, and bring quickly to the boil. After about five minutes turn down the heat and simmer for around 20 minutes. By this time the seeds should all have split. A good dodge used by many anglers is to add a little bicarbonate of soda or sugar to the water as the hemp is cooking. This helps to darken the seeds so making the white shoot more outstanding. When all the seeds have split, drain off the water and the bait is ready for use.

The easiest way to put hempseed on the hook is to press the gape into the centre of the kernel with the point at the side of the shoot. If the seed is squeezed lengthways as the hook is being inserted, the operation is made easier and there is less chance of splitting the husk.

Another method is to pass the point of the hook through the kernel and out through the bottom of the husk turning the hook at the same time so that the point protrudes upwards at the side of the shoot. Size 18 or 16 hooks are about right for hempseed though don't be afraid to scale down if there are good roach in the swim.

Fed loose, at regular intervals, hemp soon attracts fish, but they often take 'on the drop' resulting in sharp hard-to-hit bites. A better way is to keep the shoal on the bottom by adding seeds to a little groundbait. Bites then are much more positive, making it easier to connect.

Maggots

Although the humble maggot is often scorned by specimen or big fish hunters there is no doubt that it is a fine canal bait that attracts all species, which is obviously why it still ranks as the most popular bait among the majority of anglers. But for various reasons the small breeds such as 'pinkies', 'squatts', immature 'gozzers' and 'sour milk specials' are far more effective in canals than the ordinary large commercial maggot.

The 'pinkie', which is the larva of the greenbottle, is a firm favourite among match anglers, while the 'sour milk special' will often attract bites when all other baits have failed. This maggot seems to come into its own in murky industrialised canals and often lures a better stamp of fish. Unfortunately, it can only be obtained during the summer months.

'Squatts' are the larvæ of the common housefly and, being very small maggots, make excellent feeders. But two or three on the hook can make an attractive hook bait, especially for bream. Another good canal maggot is the 'gozzer' which is bred mainly by match anglers for bream and roach.

Much of the attractiveness of a maggot lies in the way it wriggles on the hook, so great care must be taken to impale it lightly through the skin so that its movements are not impeded. The best place to hook it is in the 'vent', a small piece of tissue that lies between the 'eyes' at the blunt end. If the maggot is gently squeezed, the vent protrudes and makes a perfect hooking point.

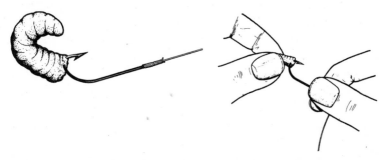

Fig 4 Maggots should always be hooked as lightly as possible leaving them the maximum amount of movement. The natural movement of the bait is one of its most attractive features

'Pinkies' Pinkies are sold at most tackle shops but it is easy, during the summer, to breed enough for a session on a canal. Homebred maggots always make better hookbaits as they are softer and more succulent, depending on the type of feed used. Only half the size of bluebottle maggots, pinkies are much livelier than other types and wriggle well on the hook, which makes them ideal for fairly still canals.

The best way to breed a controlled supply is to place a fish head or a slice of liver in a container and leave it in a sheltered spot in the garden until covered with 'fly blow' or eggs. Pinkie 'blow', the eggs of the greenbottle, are much smaller than those of the bluebottle and you can soon spot the difference when the eggs are together.

Having established which is which, scrape off a cluster of greenbottle eggs and place them on your chosen feed. This can be a dead pigeon, small chicken, a pig's heart, or a piece of fish. If a bird is used, make a deep cut in the breast in which to insert the eggs. Now place the flesh in a container, covered to prevent any flies reaching it, and leave it in a dark corner of a shed or outhouse. Inspect the flesh regularly and as soon as maggots can be seen place the container inside another one full of sawdust. If possible the second container should be put inside yet a third box, again containing sawdust. The reason for this is that pinkies have a natural tendency to migrate from the feed and exude a sticky liquid that enables them to climb the steepest and smoothest barriers.

To save going to all this trouble experienced home maggot breeders, myself included, pick off the pinkies just before they begin to leave the feed naturally, which is all a matter of timing. Fully grown fresh pinkies are white and hardly distinguishable from bluebottle maggots. In this stage they are quite deadly for bream. After two or three days they turn pink and shrink a little, but they are still very attractive.

A great advantage of pinkies is that they keep without turning into chrysalids for very long periods. In fact, I have kept them in sand for months at a time in winter. Obviously, the older they are the tougher they become, but this does not lessen their effectiveness. Fished singly or in doubles on a small hook they tempt the most finicky of fish, and, clearly, because of their small size, they make excellent loose feed. Many anglers, especially matchmen, use coloured pinkies. In fact, it is possible to buy them in varying shades, which is a bit of a contradiction in terms. Bronze, yellow and red are the most popular colours.

'Squatts' These long, yellow maggots are a traditional canal bait but are used mainly for feeding for bream and roach. In fact, Northern anglers term them 'yellow feed'. Obtainable at most tackle shops (sometimes only to order) squatts are normally stored in red foundry sand but they won't keep for long periods. Also they are susceptible to low temperatures and soon die if placed in a cold fridge. Because so few are required for canal fishing (half a pint is more than enough for one outing) it is hardly worthwhile breeding them, though this can be done easily enough with a mixture of blood and bran.

After purchasing, squatts can either be left in the sand or cleaned and stored in fine breadcrumbs. The sand is easily removed with a fine kitchen sieve but many anglers mix it in with groundbait at the waterside to add colour. Squatts can be fed loose or in groundbait depending on circumstances, but they also make a good hookbait. I know one famous match angler who uses them regularly on the hook but he always has one dead and one live one together. A foible, perhaps, but he is a man who frequently figures high in result sheets.

'Sour Bran or Milk Specials' This excellent canal bait cannot be purchased commercially but it is very easy to breed during the summer months. Larva of a large grey fly similar in size to a bluebottle, it is a pure white, large, fat maggot with soft translucent skin which is easily recognized from other types by its rounded ends. Another distinguishing feature of the 'special' is the peculiar backward movement it makes when starting to move. In fact, it actually crawls backwards for about half an inch before seeming to find its bearings to move forwards. Its natural breeding ground is in heaps of horse manure or fowl droppings, but it is also found in the bottom of pigeon nests. Active only between May and September, the fly is rarely seen but once attracted to the breeding mixture tends to stay in the area to give regular 'blows', so ensuring a constant supply of maggots.

The ingredients for the mixture that attracts the fly are bran, stale vegetable water and sour milk. A seed tray makes an idea container. This should be filled with bran that has been well dampened with stale cabbage or other vegetable water. Now pour a thick layer of sour milk (pasturised) over the bran and place the tray in a dark corner of a shed or outhouse. After a few days the sour milk will go mouldy before eventually hardening into a crust. After two weeks, carefully lift the crust and you should see small 'specials' crawling through the mixture. Usually a single blow produces only a few dozen maggots and it is rare to get more than one blow on a tray so it is difficult to breed specials in quantity.

If left, the immature maggots will eventually attain full size without any further attention but the process can be speeded up by inserting a small piece of fish or liver in the mixture below the crust. This feeds the maggots and also has an added advantage in that it attracts them into one spot, so making it easier to pick them out.

After taking the specials from the feed, wash them in a sieve under the cold water tap and store them in damp bran. The disadvantage with this maggot is that they turn to chrysalises very quickly (in two or three days in hot weather) so careful timing is necessary. Once the initial supply is established further supplies can be assured by placing a fresh tray of mixture down each week. Do not throw the old and used mixture away as it attracts a large type of housefly whose eggs grow into very large squatts, which make a good hookbait.

Fished in combination with squatts, specials are deadly for roach and bream. I find them particularly effective in the poorly stocked industrial canals of the West Midlands – waters where even a bite is sometimes an event.

'Gozzers' While the 'gozzer' is regarded perhaps more as a big water bream and roach bait, smaller versions (removed from the feed before fully grown) and mature maggots, are useful canal offerings which are very popular among match anglers.

Attractive to all species, the succulent gozzer is strictly a summer bait which cannot be purchased in the tackle shops but must be bred at home. The difference between a blue-bottle maggot and a gozzer is difficult to describe but basically the gozzer tends to be fatter in the middle and is much softer. So soft, in fact, that it will burst very easily with slight pressure which is why the fish like it so much.

The fly that produces the gozzer looks very similar to the bluebottle, but the difference is that it lays its eggs on fresh meat in darkness. This makes the breeding of gozzers fairly simple as no other flies are attracted to the breeding flesh. Pigs' and sheep's hearts, or dead birds, especially pigeons, are the most popular breeding foods.

A simple way to breed a few gozzers is to take a fresh pig's heart from the butcher's and wash it thoroughly under the cold tap. Now cut the heart open and place it, together with some clean fine sawdust, in a container. Cover the container with a lid (or newspaper) leaving just enough room for a fly to gain access to the meat, and place it in a dark sheltered spot out-of-doors. Inspect the heart every few hours until the 'blow' or eggs appear, but if none are visible within 36 hours you will have to try again with a fresh heart, otherwise ordinary bluebottles will be attracted by the smell.

As soon as a few eggs are evident, wrap the heart in a sheet of newspaper to prevent more flies reaching it and place it back in the container for the eggs to hatch. This normally takes 24 hours, and the maggots should be fully grown within three to five days depending on the weather. As I mentioned earlier, many match anglers remove the maggots before they are fully grown, as immature gozzers are very lively and therefore attractive on the hook.

Liver Maggots Maggots sold in the tackle shops are frequently referred to as liver maggots in the Midlands. But commercial maggots is a better term as I doubt whether any liver is used in breeding the thousands of gallons of bluebottle maggots that pass over tackle shop counters each week.

Actually, a maggot bred purely on liver is easily distinguishable from those fattened on the more usual fish and animal offal, as it has an attractive natural butter-yellow colour that fish find very tempting. Generally, I would never recommend commercial bluebottle maggots for canal fishing, but that's not to say they won't catch fish. They will – in certain circumstances. Gudgeon, for instance, are not too fussy about bait quality when they are feeding freely. Tench, too, are not particular about a maggot's pedigree. On the other hand, bream and roach can be very difficult to tempt with anything other than a top-class bait.

Put it this way: if no other maggots are available, use those bought from a tackle shop, but if you get a chance try the other types and see the difference.

Coloured Maggots Many canal anglers prefer coloured maggots and there is no doubt that on some canals various shades of bronze or yellow are much more effective than plain white. Pink and red are other popular colours that sometimes bring bites when other offerings are ignored.

There are two ways of colouring maggots. One is to dye the maggots externally when they are fully grown and the other is to introduce dye internally as they are feeding. While the latter method has a more permanent effect in that the dye doesn't wash off in the water, many anglers make do with the former.

Probably the quickest way to obtain a yellow shade is to dye the maggots with chrysoidine. Providing it is of the required strength (dyes come in varying degrees of potency) chrysoidine will give most shades of yellow right through to bronze, depending on the amount used and the length of time the maggots are in contact with it.

Put the maggots in a kitchen sieve and give them a thorough wash under the cold water tap. Now sprinkle a little chrysoidine powder over them and shake around for a few minutes until the dye has taken effect. Dry the maggots in fine breadcrumbs and they are ready for use.

Another method, used with less powerful dyes, is to place the maggots in a mixture of damp bran and dye powder and leave them in a warm room for a day or two until they are the required colour.

The most popular dyes are:- chrysoidine R (orange-red); chrysoidine (orange-yellow); auromine O (light yellow) and rhodamine B (pink to red). These can be obtained in powder form from most tackle shops. Another way of producing an attractive shade of yellow (but only if you breed your own hookbaits) is to introduce annatto to the feeding maggots. This is a substance used in the food industry for colouring butter, etc and many anglers prefer it to all other dyes.

Annatto is sold in solid sticks or rolls and is dark brown in colour. It is usually obtainable through adverts in the angling press. To prepare annatto simply slice off a few pieces and make these into a sloppy paste by adding a little hot water. The paste should then be smeared on the feeding material, all around the maggots preferably when they are very small.

Often, feeding maggots will try to avoid dye powders and annatto, usually in cooler weather. To encourage them ensure the container is kept warm – the higher the temperature the more ravenously maggots eat the flesh. Obviously, you must be careful not to get it too warm otherwise the maggots will sweat and die.

Breeding small quantities of hook maggots can be very interesting providing you have the necessary room to work. Bear in mind the offensive smells! Many top-class anglers are expert maggot breeders. Indeed maggot breeding is considered an important part of the sport. Often at matches there is as much rivalry with hookbaits as in the actual contest. 'What do you think of these pinkies? I bred them off a pheasant' or 'How about these sour milk specials? I coloured them with auromine', are the sort of remarks heard along the towpath.

While the pleasure or casual angler may think that maggot breeding is a messy business not worth the effort, it should be remembered that matchmen have to catch fish, frequently under poor conditions when only the best bait is good enough.

Minnows

Minnows are an excellent bait for perch and small pike, and they can be used in various ways. One of the most successful is to lip-hook a couple of lively ones and suspend them with a float in mid-water or near the bottom where they soon attract any predators in the vicinity.

While it is simple to catch a plentiful supply of minnows from most rivers during the summer months with floatfished maggots, a quick guaranteed method is to use a minnow trap. These can be purchased from some tackle dealers or made from a concave-bottomed wine bottle. There are plenty of these around and all you have to do is fill one with sand and knock a hole in the concave bottom with a metal punch. If the neck is wide it should be sealed with a piece of old net curtain or gauze to prevent the minnows escaping and that's all there is to it.

To catch the minnows, place a few pieces of bread in the

bottle and lower it into the swim (neck upstream) with a piece
of string. The minnows swim into the bottle through the hole
and then can't find their way out – it's as simple as that.

Minnows will keep for two or three days in a bucket of
water, provided they are not overcrowded, but don't throw
any dead ones away; these can be used for eel fishing.
Gudgeon also will tempt pike and perch and though perhaps
not as attractive as minnows they are much easier to keep
alive for long periods. Also, of course, they are easier to obtain
in winter.

Punched Bread
The inventive match anglers of Lancashire can take the credit
for many excellent canal methods and baits and one of their
most notable creations must be the bread punch. This device
produces pellets of bread which make an excellent bait in
clear water for small to medium sized fish.

Basically, a bread punch is a narrow, hollow metal tube
blocked off close at one end and with a sharpened inside edge
which is angled slightly inwards. This cuts and removes small
pellets from a slice of bread. The punch is speedy to use and
re-baiting the hook is simple. Also, it is a very clean method
in that the bait does not have to be handled. Because the
bread pellet is evenly compressed it stays on the hook perfectly as it swells in the water. Another advantage is that the size
of the pellet can be altered to suit the quality of the fish simply
by changing the size of the punch.

Hooks for bread-punch fishing should vary with the size of
the pellet, which can range from anything between $\frac{1}{16}$in and
$\frac{1}{2}$in. Many match anglers use a sloppy groundbait for punch
fishing, others a fine cloud, but I prefer to punch out a few
pellets and throw these in as I feel this is more natural. The
most popular punch on the market has four interchangeable
heads in different sizes but many anglers make their own. It is
most important when bread-punch fishing to have new bread.
Anything above a day old is useless, and the sliced variety is
best.

To use the punch simply place a slice of bread on a sheet of hardboard, press the punch into the bread, twist it and pull out. The hook is then inserted into the pellet of bread which comes out of the punch quite easily and cleanly. Punch fishing is a fine winter method for roach when the canals are running clear, but I never hesitate to give it a try in summer, providing the boats haven't stirred up too much mud.

Tares
Tares have accounted for many large bags of roach in rivers and they are now catching on fast as a summer and autumn canal bait. A type of bean used mainly as pigeon food, tares are cheap to buy and can be obtained from corn merchants. They are useless in their natural state though, and have to be carefully boiled until they are soft.

To prepare them for bait place a cupful (ample for a day's outing) in a saucepan of boiling water, add a pinch of bicarbonate of soda, and leave overnight. Next day, bring again to the boil and let it simmer for about an hour. The tares should be cooked by this time, but make sure by pressing one or two to see if they are soft enough for the hook. If ready, drain off the water and tip them into a clean bait tin.

A size 14 hook is about right for tares and the point should be passed through the middle and out through the side. Tares always seem to be more effective on water where hempseed is used regularly. Indeed, most anglers use the two baits in conjunction, feeding mainly hempseed and offering tares on the hook.

Wheat
Stewed, or creed, wheat is a traditional and excellent bait for several species but one that has lost much of its popularity in many parts of the country. But it is still used regularly along Midland canals during the summer and autumn, particularly on the Grand Union, where it attracts good sample fish. In fact wheat is an ideal bait for anyone anxious to avoid catching tiddlers. The one snag is that, unless it is used regularly on a water, fish are slow to become accustomed to it. In such cases, a little pre-baiting is always worthwhile and though it

sometimes takes weeks to get fish interested the end result is usually worth the trouble.

I discovered the power of wheat on canals many years ago when, flushed with my success with it on the River Severn, I decided to give it a try on the Trent and Mersey at King's Bromley. That particular summer I visited the Walsall Angling Society water three or four evenings a week, mainly with a view to improving my match fishing techniques. However, while practising various methods with maggots in different swims, I also fed an occasional few grains of wheat and gave it a try on the hook at odd intervals.

Looking back I can recall it took several visits, spread over two or three weeks, before I got my first bite on wheat. This turned out to be a roach of about half a pound, a welcome change from the tiny, stunted creatures I was used to catching. With confidence gained from that first roach I spent more and more time fishing wheat and, although it was a slow game compared with maggot fishing, I caught some fair bags of quality fish, including a few bream.

Advantages of stewed wheat are that it is inexpensive, easy to prepare and only a little is required for a day's fishing. Two cupfuls is plenty for a canal session. Many anglers have trouble putting a grain of wheat on the hook and this is probably because they try to pass the point right through each side of the outer skin, with the result that the grain breaks. The best way, I find, is to press the hook (size 14 is ideal) into the white kernel and leave it at that. If the wheat is cooked to the right texture the hook will stay put.

To prepare the wheat place two cupfuls (or more if required) into a saucepan, adding plenty of water, and bring to the boil. Now let it simmer for about an hour, or until the grains are soft and split open. Drain off the hot water and the wheat is ready for use.

Another method is to cook the wheat overnight in a vacuum flask. Place the wheat in a large flask, cover with boiling water, allowing room for expansion, and replace the stopper. The wheat will be ready for use next morning. Stewed wheat will keep for weeks in a fridge, so enough for several outings can be cooked at one time and used as and when required. If wheat is not fridged, however, it goes sour in a few days.

Worms

A worm is a deadly bait for all species of fish – big and small on all types of water – and canals are no exception. Bream, tench, roach, perch, rudd, carp and even pike find them a tasty meal, so it is wise policy to carry a supply on every visit if only as a change of bait to your usual offerings.

There are three main types of worm used as bait: lobworms (the long, slimy creatures found in the garden or on the lawn), brandlings (a wiry worm about two or three inches long, distinguished by several yellow bands on its body) and small red worms about the same size as brandlings but a deeper red in colour.

Small reds are the most popular of the three and, though they attract all species, they are normally associated with roach and bream. Brandlings are effective for perch and tench while lobworms are useful for specimen-sized fish of all species but especially for eels. The tail or head of a lobworm is also a good bait for roach, bream and perch.

Most tackle shops supply worms in cartons and these are usually brandlings. However, it is a simple task to collect your own supply, or to breed them. Brandlings and small reds will breed freely in a heap of old kitchen refuse made up of rotting cabbage leaves, potato peelings, tea leaves etc., but you will need an initial supply to start off with. These can be found in mature manure heaps, their natural habitat.

Lobworms can be picked off close-cut lawns on damp summer nights and stored in a box of damp soil and grass cuttings until required. Worms are delicate creatures and soon die if heaped together in a bait box. So carry them in a box lined with wet strips of newspsper, or better still damp sphagnum moss (sold at most florists).

It is important when hooking worms to ensure that the worm has enough freedom to wriggle invitingly, but not enough to enable it to crawl out of sight. For instance if a large lobworm is hooked through the tail only and fished on the bottom, it will most likely crawl into the mud. Therefore pass the hook through it in two or three places so that it forms a sort of loop. The same applies to the smaller red worms.

Finally on the subject of worms, I must mention the experiences of my uncle (the same one who introduced me to hempseed fishing). These days with failing eyesight, and not much energy, he is content, wherever he goes, to sling out a large lobworm and sit back and contemplate. Now, while this method ensures he has plenty of time to enjoy his surroundings, the fish he catches from local canals are usually eye-openers. On the few occasions I have accompanied him in recent years, he has caught bream to 4lb, perch to 2lb, several roach over 1lb, and a pike of 10lb. Not to mention a couple of smashes that were probably big carp.

Having seen him catch big fish I can well believe the tales he tells of outings that have produced double-figure bags. Of course he has many blank days (don't we all?) but it is certainly food for thought.

5 The Fish

Bream

Bream are widely distributed in some canals but, although the small 'skimmers' spread themselves throughout long stretches, the bigger fish tend to shoal very tightly in certain areas and are not always easy to find. However, once a shoal has been located – and a sure sign (apart from actually seeing the fish) is a patch of muddy or cloudy water where feeding bream have stirred up the canal bed while grubbing for food – you can be sure they will remain in the approximate vicinity for a long time.

Why bream prefer one small area in a long and, often, featureless stretch of water, is open to conjecture. Obviously, there must be a reason and it probably boils down to the food supply. It could be that there is an abundance of bloodworms or other creatures on which they feed. Or it could simply be the activities of anglers themselves in groundbaiting the spot regularly as, once a bream hole is discovered the word soon spreads along the grapevine. Bream 'holes', in fact, are common along many canals and huge bags are sometimes landed by those fortunate anglers who happen to pick the right spot at the right time.

I remember a large shoal in the Taunton–Bridgwater Canal, in Somerset, which stayed in exactly the same spot for at least three seasons. Local anglers, and visitors like myself, enjoyed undreamed of sport during the summer months and catches in the regions of 70lb were not unfamiliar. The bream, which must have numbered hundreds and which ranged up to 3lb, were confined in such a small weedy area that only two anglers could fish comfortably at any one time. And, despite many efforts on the part of latecomers to the spot, nothing would persuade the bream to move or spread out.

Not that bream always confine themselves to one particular area. I know several canals where the shoals are constantly on the move and they sometimes patrol very long lengths of water. In this situation the only solution is to bait up a swim and sit back hoping the bream will eventually pass by.

Some specialists pre-bait a swim for several days prior to a visit but, while this is a great help, it is not always possible. Baiting up the swim is, in fact, one of the most important parts of bream fishing and many anglers use huge quantities of cereal groundbait containing hook-bait samples. Large amounts would do more harm than good in canals though, and discretion is needed to ensure the pitch is not overfed. The best plan is to throw several small balls into the swim to form a small carpet and then wait for developments. If the bream begin feeding, throw in a little more, with as little disturbance as possible.

A dodge used by match anglers is to mix a few casters in the groundbait even when they are not used on the hook. The idea behind this (and there is evidence that it works) is that the casters encourage the bream to stay around longer.

Bream are warm-weather feeders generally, but enough are caught in winter to refute any suggestion that they hibernate. Indeed, it is possible to take large catches from some waters on very cold days. But as a rule these fish are taken from the shelter of deep water swims which, unfortunately, are non-existent in canals. But, even though few good-sized bream are caught from canals in winter, the smaller fish can be very active during the milder spells, as match anglers will confirm.

Like most still-water fish, bream feed mainly at dawn and dusk, and sometimes through the night. But this shouldn't deter a daytime visitor as they can invariably be persuaded to feed on the brightest days by the careful use of groundbait. If I was restricted to one particular bait for canal bream I would choose bread in some form every time. It is a bait that rarely fails no matter what mood the fish are in, and what's more it attracts bigger specimens. Maggots, casters and worms may be equally effective on occasions, and perhaps even better in coloured water. They also offer a better chance of tempting small fish, but for sheer consistency bread is unbeatable.

While bream grow to sizeable proportions in lakes and rivers, the canal variety rarely exceed 4lb with an average of much less. A three-pounder can be considered a good fish at anytime, but several canals have produced five and six-pounders over the years.

Regardless of their size still-water bream never put up much of a fight so strong tackle is unnecessary unless the water happens to be very weedy. This is fortunate in one respect as bream are sometimes tackle-shy, which calls for small hooks and fine line.

Floatfishing is the best method for canal bream: a light 12-foot rod is ideal for most situations. Legering tactics are necessary on occasions and then an eight or nine-foot legering rod with a small swing tip is needed. Reel line of 2½lb breaking strain with hook lengths of 1½ to 2lb breaking strain is strong enough for open type water. Weedy swims would probably call for 3 or 4lb reel line and 2½lb bottoms to make sure of landing a decent sized fish.

While it always pays to match the hook to the bait it is often better to scale down a size for bream, particularly on hard-fished waters where they become educated to tackle. This applies principally when using casters, maggots or worms, and perhaps is not quite so important with bread-flake. Nevertheless, most successful bream anglers tend to use comparatively small hooks, such as size 14, for breadflake, and 16s and 18s for maggots and casters. These are usually tied to fine nylon to ensure the maximum number of bites. On the other hand I can recall a day when I finished up using size 12s tied direct to my reel line to take a fair net of bream from the Shropshire Union Canal. But this was one of those occasions when the fish seemed blind to everything except the bait.

A still bait, presented hard on the bottom, is the basic formula for successful bream fishing and, while legering is the most popular method on deep rivers and lakes, float tactics are simpler and more effective for canals. The exceptions are when there is a very strong pull on the water, such as in rough weather, or when it is too dark to see a float.

Laying on, or lightly anchoring both the bait and the float to the bottom is a favourite float method for bream. It is a simple rig and most floats, other than sticks or the loaded variety, are suitable. The float is fastened by the bottom ring only, about six to 12inches over-depth, with the shot placed in a bunch, say a foot from the hook. The tackle is cast beyond the baited area and the bait slowly dragged into position while gradually tightening the line until just the tip of the float protrudes above the surface. The rod is then placed in a rest. If there is any current or pull on the water, it is better to fasten the float top and bottom to prevent it being dragged under.

Bites with this set-up are usually quite positive, but watch out for lift bites as bream often pick up the shot as they take the bait, which results in the float rising up in the water. If the bottom is weedy, keep the amount of lead shot to a minimum and place it well away from the hook, otherwise it will drag the bait into the weed. When the pull on the canal is exceptionally strong, use a bulkier float and replace the lead shot with a small drilled bullet stopped with a dust shot and you have an effective float-leger rig.

In very windy conditions on open water, light legering tackle, together with a small swing tip, will give better bite indication. But keep the leger weight as small as possible – it should be fastened to the reel line with a short nylon link – and set the rod as near parallel with the bank as you can get it.

Carp

Carp were comparatively rare in our canals until recent times but, thanks to re-stocking operations carried out by the British Waterways Board, Water Authorities, angling associations and clubs, they are becoming widespread. Fast-growing fish, and easily the most powerful of our still water species, they soon reach double-figure proportions if enough food is available.

Many carp in the teens of pounds have been landed and 20-pounders are on record from certain canals, not to mention a huge fish of 31½lb landed from the Grand Union in 1975. Carp are generally summer feeders, most active during darkness or on hot overcast days. Their normal diet is a mixture of small aquatic insects such as shrimps and bloodworms, together with weed and water plants.

Although they obtain most of their food off the bottom, they also rise to the surface to suck in any likely morsels and the sound they make when doing this is unmistakable. In fact, the 'clooping' or 'chomping' of carp, as it is called by the specialist carp hunters, is a sure giveaway to their presence in a water. Intelligent, and cunning to a degree, carp can be very difficult (but paradoxically very easy) to catch, usually depending on the amount of angling activity carried out.

Once hooked they are in a class of their own and put up a fight the like of which no angler is likely to forget. I know I shall always remember the exciting tussles I used to have with quite small carp, around the four and five pound mark, in a disused arm of a now abandoned and dried up canal in Shropshire. I used to catch these fish with freelined floating bread crust as dusk was falling and they ran off like express trains as soon as they felt the hook. I never landed more than three in a session and the more I tried the more difficult they became to tempt. It finally reached the stage where they would take every piece of crust I threw in – except for the one on the hook. But I found it so exciting that I kept trying night after night even though a round trip of 60 miles was involved.

Incidentally, I tried many other different methods and baits to catch them but I was only ever successful with crust. Carp, in fact, will accept many other baits, such as maggots, casters, worms, boiled potato, cheese etc., providing they are reasonably accustomed to them. I say reasonably in the sense that, being intelligent fish, carp soon learn to associate certain baits with danger. In other words, the more a bait is used the less the chances become of hooking a carp with it. This is not a hard and fast rule by any means as there will always be exceptions, but it should certainly be borne in mind.

Finding carp in canals is not an easy task as they tend to wander a great deal, but fortunately back and forth within certain limits. Usually they inhabit the most weedy stretches where they can sometimes be seen basking near the surface on hot days. One way of locating them is to listen for the noise they make when surface feeding, but often the only clue is via the local grapevine or the angling press.

Since they are most likely to be found in the weedy areas and because of their great strength, carp tackle needs to be very powerful. Although I used to get away with 4lb breaking strain line and an ordinary 12-foot general purpose rod for those small Shropshire fish, it was sometimes touch and go trying to keep them out of the weed. And if there had been any slightly larger carp in the stretch I wouldn't have hesitated in scaling up to 10lb line and a stout carp rod, for once carp get among the weed they become virtually immovable as they twist in and out, wrapping the line around the thick stalks.

To illustrate this I have only to relate the experiences of Geoff Franks, formerly a noted canal carp specialist from Bromsgrove, Worcs. Geoff has dozens of sizeable fish to his credit from the Birmingham–Worcester Canal. He once landed eight to 10lb in one day – no mean feat in such a narrow, shallow and confined water. Living close to the canal Geoff had an advantage in that he was able to watch out for cruising carp and note the areas in which they spent most time. Then, when weather conditions were suitable, he made his attack – usually early in the morning or early evening.

His tackle consisted of a powerful two-piece carp rod, a fixed spool reel loaded with 12lb breaking strain line with a size 2 straight-eyed carp hook tied direct. For bait he rarely used anything but floating breadcrust and he always freelined it. After creeping as quietly as possible to his chosen pitch (always where there was a thick bed of rushes on the far side) Geoff cast the crust across the canal right into the middle of the rushes. Then by manipulating the rod, he would jerk the crust on to the surface of the water. On one occasion a carp actually came up and took the crust while it was hanging an inch from the water. Geoff never pre-baited or threw in any extra pieces of crust as attractors as, knowing the carp were there anyway and that they liked bread crust, he reckoned this increased his chances of getting a take.

When a carp sucked in the crust Geoff reacted like lightning with a hefty strike and quickly dragged the carp from the rushes into clear water to play it into the net. Geoff says that he would probably have had more takes if he'd used finer tackle but then he wouldn't have been able to apply the amount of pressure needed to force even small fish out of weed. He also caught carp on freelined breadflake, lobworms, luncheon meat and cheese paste off the bottom, but he still maintains that floating crust is the deadliest bait of all for canal carp.

Eels

All canals contain their quota of eels and though the majority caught are usually on the small side, enough four, five and six-pounders have been landed to suggest that there are more big ones than most anglers suspect.

Eels are not a popular fish except among a few specialists. In fact, most anglers hate them because they swallow baits intended for other species and because they make such a mess of one's tackle, snagging or tangling it up as they try to wriggle free, and covering everything in slime if they are landed. Little wonder that they are stamped into the ground or have their heads chopped off by irate captors. As one writer once said 'Killing an eel is a protracted business for the eel is composed largely of slime and immortality.' Yet, if taken seriously, eel fishing can provide pretty good sport and quite a few thrills, particularly when a big one is hooked.

Finding eels is a chancy business as normally they frequent areas where deeper water, underwater obstacles such as sunken trees and other debris, or holes in banks, offer protection. There are few such spots in canals, though the water immediately underneath and around bridges where brick and stonework has fallen in has proved fruitful along the Birmingham–Worcester and Grand Union Canals. The Grand Union, incidentally, has yielded some very big specimens from near bridges, including a monster of 8lb 7oz.

Famous big fish specialist Bob Church, from Northampton, and his friends first realised the potential of the Grand Union as a big eel water. Concentrating, in 1965, on a length near Northampton for a whole summer, the group landed several over five pounds, Bob himself notching up eels of 4¾lb, 5¼lb and 5½lb. Bob's favourite bait, by the way, was double lobworm anchored over a groundbait mixture of raw eggs and pilchard oil thickened with fine soil.

Eel fishing canals is a matter of trial and error – a case of experimenting in different areas until the fish are located. The Northampton Specimen Group averaged something like 100 hours per eel on their forays along the Grand Union. Pre-baiting a specific spot can help. Small dead fish such as gudgeon, bleak and minnows, or chopped up lobworms thrown into a likely swim a day or two before a session often attract eels as they have a keen sense of smell. Lobworms or dead fish are, in fact, the most popular hook baits for eels.

The most favourable time to fish for eels is during the summer months after dark – if night fishing is allowed, that is. Otherwise very early morning or as dusk is falling are the most profitable hours, as the bigger specimens usually hide up during the day.

Tackle for eels needs to be much stronger than that used for other species of comparable weight as, besides being very powerful, eels have a nasty knack of wrapping themselves, and the line, around the nearest obstacle if given the slightest leeway. They also have strong teeth and have been known to bite through thick nylon. For this reason they have to be dragged from the water as quickly as possible without any ceremony as soon as they are hooked. To do this a stout carp-type rod, and line of at least 7lb breaking strain are necessary, plus a good strong hook. Most anglers tie their hooks direct to the reel line for eel fishing in order to eliminate any weaknesses caused through knots or loops. But if a trace is preferred it should be of the same breaking strain as the reel line or even stronger. In fact, some eel specialists use a wire trace.

Hooks need to be on the large side and size 4 or 6 are ideal for a bunch of lobworms, while trebles of the same sizes are better for dead-bait fishing.

There is little to choose between these two baits for eels, and each have their devotees. Dead fish are perhaps the most widely used but there is some evidence to suggest that more big eels are tempted with a bunch of lobworms than with dead fish. Also it should be remembered that eels have very small mouths and can swallow worms more easily.

Leger weights or lead shot are unnecessary unless a float is used because a bunch of lobworms or a dead fish is heavy enough to cast the short distance required and, of course, there is no current to disturb the bait once it reaches the canal bottom. Weightless tackle can be an advantage too as, contrary to belief, eels (big ones that is) can be wary at times and soon drop a bait if they feel resistance. For this reason also, the bale arm of the reel should be left open to allow the line to run off freely.

Bites are easily recognisable with or without a float as, normally, when an eel picks up the bait it swims off a short distance and then stops to swallow it. This is the best time to strike the hook home but if there are snags in the swim it is unwise to wait, so it pays to strike after a short interval while the eel is still running, and as soon as resistance is felt as much pressure as possible should be applied to bring the eel in.

There is little point in returning eels alive as they do more harm than good, but killing them need not be the messy business most anglers make it. Eel hunters have discovered that if an eel is laid on its back in a furrow it will lie there quite still until it dies. A strange phenomenon it's true – but it works every time.

Gudgeon

Gudgeon are such small creatures that they are of interest only to match anglers, or pike enthusiasts who use them for live-bait. Yet, for their size, gudgeon are bonny little fighters and provide good sport if very light tackle is used. I include the species in this book for the simple reason that they are so prolific in many Northern and Midland canals that they cannot be ignored. The Staffs–Worcester Canal in particular is thick with them in certain areas as are the Oxford and Grand Union Canals.

Gudgeon are greedy little fish that feed all the year round, at all times of the day, no matter how cold or hot, and often they will take a bait the moment it hits the bottom. Strictly bottom-feeders, they are normally found at the edges of a canal, generally moving to the middle in the winter.

Maggots, bloodworms and small pieces of breadflake are the best baits to catch them though they will take other offerings provided they are small enough. They are very fond of cereal groundbait which should be heavily mixed to concentrate a shoal in a small area.

Match anglers are adept at catching gudgeon and often whip out three or four hundred in a three-hour match. They normally use a short roach pole (about nine foot long) with a size 20 or 18 hook baited with a single pinkie maggot and a loaded float carrying one single shot near the hook.

Small pieces of groundbait containing squatts are thrown into the swim at regular intervals depending on how the gudgeon are feeding, and from then on it is simply a case of lifting gudgeon out at every cast. It is not everybody's idea of angling, but it is better than catching nothing at all, and of course there is always the chance that a bigger fish will grab the bait.

Perch

Perch are found in most canals but they rarely grow to any great size and a two-pounder is considered a remarkable fish. There are exceptions, however, as with all species, and perch up to 3½lb (outstanding by any standards) are landed from time to time. In fact, I remember a period in the '60s when two and three-pounders were so common in certain lengths of the Staffs–Worcester Canal near Stafford that some match anglers abandoned their traditional tiddler-snatching methods and fished for perch with lobworms – often quite successfully.

At that time perch were prolific all over the country and frequently outnumbered all species except roach in most canals. But the shoals were ravaged later by an unknown disease which drastically reduced stocks. Now the perch are gradually returning and, if all goes well, it shouldn't be too long before they again become well established.

Hardy fish that feed all the year round, even on the coldest days, perch seem most active in late summer and autumn when they often swallow baits intended for other species. Perch swim around and feed in shoals and these nearly always consist of similar sized fish, probably from the same spawn. But, being cannibals, they eat each other until only a few survive. Which is no doubt why the size of a shoal varies in proportion to the size of the fish. In other words, the smaller the perch, the larger the shoal, and vice versa. Perch can usually be found all along canals so it is difficult to pinpoint spots where they are most likely to be.

Favourite perch haunts in the summer and autumn are around spawning beds such as rushes, as they feed regularly on fry. In fact, it is a common sight to see perch chasing fry across the surface. The deeper areas, if any, are sometimes productive later in the year, especially if the bottom is clean or gravelly; while holes or open spaces among weedy stretches can also be rewarding. Generally though, locating perch in canals is more a matter of luck than judgment and experience along a particular length of water the only guide.

Pre-baiting with chopped worms can help, as I once discovered by chance on the Trent and Mersey Canal near Lichfield. In search of tench, I had pre-baited a pitch with hundreds of chopped worms prior to the opening of the season. I arrived at the swim full of expectancy at the crack of dawn on opening day and baited my hook with a brandling. But when my float dipped for the first time out came a small perch of about 6oz. Dozens more of the same size followed that morning but not one tench showed. So much for pre-baiting with chopped worms, I thought.

Perch, in fact, although predators and cannibals are gluttons for worms of all kinds. Hang a juicy lobworm in mid-water and they just can't resist it. Maggots too, or anything that wriggles, are just as deadly at times, though to tempt the really big perch small live-baits or spinners are a better bet. Minnows are in a class of their own for live-baiting, and gudgeon or small roach will do at a pinch.

It might be imagination (there is no evidence to prove it) but perch appear to be attracted by red baits. Tackle for perch should be light but on the strong side as they are bonny fighters. True, they never seem sure which way to turn and usually end up swimming round in circles, but they certainly pull hard.

A general purpose rod with plenty of action and 2- to 3-pound reel line will give plenty of control for floatfishing and live-baiting, while the same line with a small (6- or 7-foot) spinning rod will ensure the utmost enjoyment from a spinning session.

When floatfishing, the bait can be presented on or off the bottom because perch, being predators, tend to swim at all depths. Generally speaking, a bait suspended off the bottom seems more effective in canals but there is no hard-and-fast rule. Much depends on the clarity of the water and the type of bottom, because perch find most of their food by sight and vibration rather than by smell, therefore it often pays to keep the bait on the move by jerking the rod tip at regular intervals.

Groundbaiting for perch with chopped up worms, or breadcrumbs and maggots, is frequently beneficial, particularly the latter as this attracts small roach which in turn attract perch. Perch are not tackle-shy so there is no need to use small hooks. Size 14 or 16 are suitable for maggots and 12 and 10 suitable for worms, and they can be tied direct to the reel line. When live-baiting a minnow or other small fish it should be hooked through the top lip and suspended between bottom and mid-water with as small a float as possible.

A size 8 or 10 hook is plenty big enough and a single swan shot will hold the minnow in position. But, as with other baits, it should be kept constantly on the move by jerking the float if necessary. Once the live-bait has been worked through

the swim a few times (as near as possible to any weed beds) it
is best to try a different spot. Perch are not slow to take a bait
once they catch sight of it so there is little point in hanging
around too long unless it happens to be a recognised perchy
area.

Pike

Pike haunt most clear water canals and though they are
generally on the small side double-figure fish are captured
occasionally and 20-pounders are not unknown. Few anglers
specialise in pike fishing along canals, however, as the fish are
often thinly spread and difficult to locate. They can sometimes be spotted basking near the surface on a summer's day
but more often than not the only clue to their presence is
when they attack and scatter the shoal of fish you happen to
be catching. Consequently it pays to be prepared and to carry
pike gear on every visit. Of course, once you know that a pike
is present in a specific area you can make a return visit
because they usually stay for long periods. Also it's a safe bet
that there may be one or two around as they frequently hunt
in groups.

The weedy stretches of canals are favourite haunts of pike
because this is where their staple diet (other fish) is likely to
be. Pike like to lie in hiding, waiting for their prey to come
close enough for an easy capture. Sometimes, though, they
have to go out in search of food which is when they usually
reveal themselves to the angler.

The winter months are the traditional times for pike fishing. This is when pike are supposed to be in top fighting trim
and when they feed most. That's not to say they don't feed all
the year round and I must admit the many pike I have caught
in the summer seemed quite fit and always fought well for
their freedom.

I shall never forget a tussle I had with a ten-pounder one
hot July day along the Taunton–Bridgwater Canal. I was
busy catching roach and rudd when the first pike showed and
I wasted no time in rigging up some tackle. I didn't have the
proper pike gear with me so I simply tied a size 2 hook to 5lb

reel line and lip-hooked a small rudd. I suspended the fish a couple of feet below a large chub float with three swan shot to hold it down towards the bottom and threw it to the middle of the canal.

I didn't have to wait long before the float disappeared and the tremendous battle began. The pike actually leapt from the water a couple of times but I couldn't apply much pressure as I was only using a light general purpose rod. Fortunately, the pike swam round in circles and didn't attempt to run, and I eventually landed it. I suppose I was lucky in a way, though I felt quite pleased with myself for capturing the fish on make-shift tackle. Of course, if the pike had ventured into the weed it would most likely have escaped which is why I now make it my business to carry proper pike tackle on most outings.

Tackle for canal pike need not be anywhere near so power-ful as that required on larger waters, for the chances of hooking a monster are pretty remote. Nevertheless it is fool-hardy to scale down too fine so it is best to compromise. A light eight or nine foot spinning rod, and line between 7 and 10lb breaking strain can be used for both spinning and plug fishing as well as live and dead-baiting. Traces should be made from Alasticum wire (pike have very sharp teeth) and fastened to the line by a small swivel. While treble hooks fastened singly or in tandem fashion offer a better chance of hooking a pike, many anglers use single hooks for live-baiting because they are less likely to damage the fish.

The traditional pike bung, or float, is far too bulky for canal fishing and completely unnecessary as the bait is usually on the small side and never very far away. An ordinary, extra-large, balsa float will support a live-bait and, what's more, offers much less resistance when a pike takes. Baits for pike vary from live fish through a wide range of spinners and plugs to dead-baits such as sprats and mackerel. But while all these can be used in canals they should be scaled down consider-ably to match the size of the pike. I have only tried dead-baiting a few times and then I used a dead gudgeon in preference to a sprat, but without success I should add. In their feeding habits pike are very unpredictable fish. They have no set pattern of feeding and can never be relied upon to take a bait no matter how ideal the conditions may seem. Sometimes they appear ravenous and attack everything that moves while on other occasions they lie motionless ignoring all offerings. Therefore it would be foolish to try and lay down any rules as to when and how to catch them. Mild winter days reputedly offer the best chances on most waters and generally this applies to canals. Certainly I have had little success in very cold weather and I think the reason for this is that canals being shallow are particularly susceptible to air temperatures and become too cold even for pike. Of the many methods for catching pike live-baiting is possibly the most productive in canals. Spinning and plug fishing are also rewarding, however, and certainly more popular on colder days providing a chance to keep on the move. But a good dodge practised in the Midlands is to combine both methods by tethering a live-bait and then spinning towards it.

Roach
Roach are the most commonplace species in canals and although millions were killed by the diseases that swept the country in the late '60s they are gradually returning in large numbers. Hardy fish that feed freely and thrive in most conditions, the canal variety rarely grow to much above a pound, though specimens over two pounds have been recorded, sometimes from the most unlikely canals.

Before disease struck, most Midland and Northern Canals were full of small, stunted roach, no larger than a cigarette, and these could be a nuisance. They grabbed every bait they could find. Since they were wiped out, the chances of contacting better class fish have greatly increased. Indeed, it is very noticeable that the average stamp of present day canal roach is much better than ten years ago.

They will accept most baits, but casters, maggots, bread in some form, and seed baits such as hemp, tares and wheat, are the most popular. However, if big fish are the target, a lobworm or a lump of breadflake takes some beating as Albert Oldfield proved along the Macclesfield Canal some years ago when he landed many roach between two and three pounds on flake and lobworms. Cheese is another good bait for the big ones – I have had several around the 1½lb mark on a knob of Edam.

It's been said that an angler who can catch roach consistently from hard-fished water is a master of his craft. This is because roach tend to become tackle-shy and refuse any bait that doesn't behave perfectly naturally. This certainly applies on canals, particularly those that are match-fished. Even the small roach sometimes bite short and nibble the end of the maggot or caster, so it's little wonder that roach fishing has become synonymous with fine tackle. Unless your target is a real big 'un it pays to use the finest lines and smallest hooks possible. Canal roach cannot exactly be described as powerful fish and they tend to swim around in circles when hooked, so it's not too difficult to land good samples on frail hook lengths and reel lines. Most experts seem to prefer 1lb breaking strain bottoms tied to 1½lb reel line. Unless the swim is very weedy you will need nothing stronger than 1½lb bottoms.

As for hooks, the smaller they are the more bites you will get, though, obviously they should match the size of the bait. Sizes 18 and 20 are ideal for maggots, but a 16, or even a 14, can sometimes be buried out of sight inside a chrysalis and will offer a better chance of hooking the fish. For large pieces of breadflake or lobworms, when pursuing specimens, size 12 or 10 are more suitable.

Floats need to be extra sensitive for roach for they are apt to suck in and mouth a bait with hardly any movement of the line or float. Darts and loaded antennas are useful for close range tactics, while for laying on and trotting the flow stick floats come into their own. Windy conditions demand more buoyant quills, which can be shotted to help better bait control. For laying on or trotting the current when the wind is in the same direction, a more natural bait presentation can be achieved by fishing 'peg leg' – that is fastening the float by the bottom ring only. This method enables the line to be kept below the surface to overcome any drag caused by the wind. It also aids quieter casting and striking.

Roach tend to feed on shelves of canals, quite close to the bank at times depending on weed growth, and one of the deadliest methods in all conditions is to offer casters well across, laid hard on the bottom. A stick float, fastened top and bottom and set at a couple of feet more than the depth is perfect for this. One or two shot should be placed 12 to 18 inches from the hook. The size of these can be altered to ensure the bait is kept still for, being on the bottom, they won't affect the trimming of the float. The remainder of the shot are placed just off bottom.

Another way of offering the bait in a similar manner when the wind is troublesome is with an antenna or waggler float (five or six inches long) locked on the reel line with, say, a couple of BB shot, and with a couple of dust shot below and maybe another two above the float (or back shotted) to help sink the line.

The same rigs, with variations in floats, shot etc., can be employed for other baits for fishing the middle and close in. Feeding for the still-bait style should be as sparse as possible, a sprinkling of loose hook baits, at long intervals, is sufficient.

When maggots are preferred, the more succulent and smaller variety such as sour milk specials, pinkies, squatts and gozzers are far more effective than the commerical type and should be offered just touching bottom and kept on the move by manipulating the rod tip. This attracts the roach more often than not, but they have a tendency to refuse moving baits at times, in which case the float should be raised slightly to allow the bait to rest on the canal bed (not for too long, though, as maggots are apt to crawl out of sight).

Rigs for this type of fishing are legion. My own choice, which I think takes some beating, is a dart or small antenna trimmed by one small shot. Feeding, when maggot fishing, is best done on the 'little and often' principle using lightly mixed groundbait laced with squatts or pinkies.

Hempseed is a deadly bait for roach during the summer, and it invariably attracts a better class of fish. In fact, roach like hempseed so much they often rise to the surface to grab any loose offerings. I remember many occasions, on a heavily hemp-fished stretch of the Trent and Mersey Canal, when they came to the top in anticipation even when I just went through the motions of throwing in the seed.

When this happens bites can be too sharp to hit though, so to keep the roach down I prefer to feed the hemp in small lumps of groundbait, and offer the hook bait just touching bottom. A small dart float trimmed with a 'mouse dropping' shot or a Continental 'STYLE' lead, or a tiny twist of lead wire, will eliminate false bites which occur when fish grab the shot thinking it is a grain of hemp.

Incidentally, casters work well in conjunction with hemp-seed. Many anglers feed with hemp and put a single caster on the hook and the roach don't seem to mind. But, while hemp-seed is best fished 'on the drop', or just touching bottom, wheat and tares are more effective when 'laid on' as still as possible, similar to casters. Not that casters can't be fished 'on the drop' or move. On the contrary, roach will take them off the surface in the summer and the method described under 'Rudd' has accounted for many a good catch.

Rudd

Although rudd are very similar to roach in appearance and habits they are by no means as common in our canals. But where they are well established they sometimes outnumber the roach. The two species are often confused but there are two marked differences which should always clear up any doubt. First, the rudd's bottom lip protrudes slightly beyond the top lip, while the reverse applies to the roach. And second-ly, the rudd's dorsal fin is placed much nearer the tail. Also the rudd is much more brightly coloured than the roach. Generally rudd grow larger than roach and two-pounders are fairly common. But they average much less in canals and most shoals I have encountered have consisted of 4 to 6oz fish, plus odd bigger specimens around the 1lb mark.

Rudd seem to thrive in very weedy, clear-water canals, which is probably why they are rare in the Midlands and the North where most waterways are continually coloured by the passing of boats. Although rudd will feed all the year round they are most active during the summer months when large shoals can often be seen cruising and feeding near the surface. In fact, this is where the rudd really differs from the roach in that it often feeds off the bottom, a habit the angler can use to his advantage by catching them with the deadly 'on the drop' or falling bait method. But don't get the impression that rudd never feed on the canal bed. They do, and I have caught plenty with a well anchored bait. It mainly depends on the weather: if it is cold the rudd keep their heads down, and if it is warm they come up to the surface.

Rudd will feed at all hours of the day and night during the summer, even at mid-day when the sun is blazing down. But they are not bold fish and the big ones rarely leave the cover of the weed beds until the sun has gone down. The small ones can easily be tempted out, however, with a little cloud-bait and a few maggots to provide sport when most other species are lying low.

Baits for rudd are more or less the same as for roach but with the accent on the slow-sinking varieties. In addition, breadcrust and floating casters or chrysalids are deadly during the summer and will often tempt the bigger fish on the surface.

Tackle should be more or less the same as for roach, too, though larger hooks and stronger line can be used for rudd are seldom tackle-shy. While they can be caught with roach methods on the bottom, a favourite style is to tempt them in mid-water or near the surface with a falling bait, and the nearer you cast to a weed bed the better your chances are of hooking a better-class fish.

A loaded float, heavy enough to enable accurate casting to the edges of or even in the open spaces among weed beds, is essential for this method. The float should be attached by the bottom ring only. This reduces the likelihood of tangles while casting. Set it at the approximate depth of the water and place the single shot about a foot from the hook. A little lightly-mixed groundbait, as used by match anglers, is ideal to get rudd interested and a few samples of the hook bait should be mixed in each portion. Throw in a few small lightly-squeezed balls around the weeds at the start and then regulate your offerings according to how the rudd are feeding.

When using this slow-sinking bait method, bites are indicated either by the float failing to settle correctly or lifting slightly as the fish holds up the shot. Of course if you don't strike at this moment the float will eventually dip, but by this time the fish may have swallowed the bait. The same tackle minus the shot, and with the hook length greased to help it float, can be used to tempt rudd off the surface.

Floating casters or small pieces of breadcrust are good baits for this method, which can be deadly at times. If the rudd are not already near the surface a few floating casters or bits of crust should be scattered over a wide area to attract them. Another way to present a bait near the surface is to attach a small, ¼in diameter, polystyrene ball about six inches from the hook. Just make a slit in it with a razor blade and slide it on the line. The same loaded float can be used, but extra weight to aid casting can be added by placing a small shot each side of the ball. Bites for both these methods can be spotted by watching the line near the bait rather than the float. As soon as you see it run across the surface, lift the rod to drive the hook home.

Tench

Tench thrive in shallow, weedy, water and for this reason some canals, particularly those that are little used and remain undisturbed by boats, hold quite a large head. But they are by no means a common fish and the shoals, even when well established, are usually thinly spread over a long length of water.

Generally, canal tench don't grow to any great size, 2lb is about average, but larger fish up to 6lb turn up regularly in some waters. Usually, their individual size depends on the numbers of fish in a given area: the more numerous the tench the smaller the average size seems to be, due no doubt to the supply of food available.

For instance, the Staffs–Worcester Canal and the Trent and Mersey support reasonable-sized shoals of tench in isolated spots but their average size is only about 1lb. On the other hand, tench are spread fairly evenly throughout the Taunton–Bridgwater Canal in Somerset and, though few in number, they grow quite large, averaging between 3 and 5lb. But many specimen tench, in excess of 6lb, have been landed from canals.

Finding tench in canals is not easy for they rarely surface and show themselves during the day except when they are spawning, which is sometimes as late as the end of July. On these occasions the shoals are easily spotted as they roll and cavort in the weed. Otherwise the only sign that they are present is in the streams of tiny bubbles (almost like froth) which they expel as they root in the mud for bloodworms and snails etc. Tench bubbles, in fact, are something of a pheno-menon which, once seen, cannot be mistaken for anything else.

When a shoal have got their heads down in the mud the surface erupts with bubbles and the movements of individual fish can be followed from the trail of bubbles moving up and down the canal.

A habit of canal tench, favourable to the angler, is that like bream the shoals stay in the same localised areas year after year. For this reason the best tench swims are usually well known to regular visitors on most canals. Before fishing strange waters it therefore pays to make a few discreet enquiries among the local anglers.

I have enjoyed some excellent tench fishing on the Taunton–Bridgwater while on holiday thanks to help from anglers in the Bridgwater district. The tench is a summer feeder that rarely shows in canals after October though, as with all other species, there are exceptions to the rule and the odd one turns up occasionally during the winter. June, July and August are the most favourable months, especially if there is a hot spell. But though they love warm water tench are not fond of sunlight and feed mainly at dawn and dusk, sometimes during the night or in very overcast conditions.

Probably the most popular hour for tench fishing is at day-break when the water is perfectly still and a mist is rising. At such a time it can be very exciting, waiting for a motionless float to disappear out of sight, or watching the myriads of tiny bubbles bursting on the surface. But these are the golden moments and I must confess I have had better sport when the surface has been ruffled by strong winds. In fact, judging the right conditions for tench fishing is not easy because they are unpredictable fish which often fail to put in an appearance when everything seems right. But then again when they are feeding they can be very easy to catch.

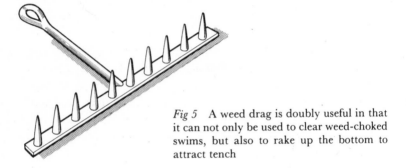

Fig 5 A weed drag is doubly useful in that it can not only be used to clear weed-choked swims, but also to rake up the bottom to attract tench

One method, used by many tench anglers to induce them to feed, is to drag out a swim with a rake thus removing the weed and stirring up the mud. Half an hour spent doing this can be quite profitable and there is no need to wait for the water to settle afterwards for the operation actually attracts the tench into the area. And if two or three handfuls of maggots or casters are thrown into the swim while raking is in progress and raked into the mud they will serve as excellent bait attractors.

Tench are very fond of maggots and casters but other firm favourites are lobworms and brandlings and various forms of bread. They are not generally tackle-shy, except in some hard-fished match lengths, which is fortunate as they are powerful fish which take some stopping once they get the feel of the hook. Consequently tackle should be stout enough to be able to apply plenty of pressure when they head for the weed – which they invariably do. Three or 4lb reel line with the hook tied direct or to a slightly weaker trace, is sufficient for most swims. But if there are lily pads in the vicinity it pays to use something stronger as these plants have rather tough stems which can be a match for even 7lb line.

The rod should have enough power to stop the tench dead in its tracks if necessary. Though many good-sized fish have been landed with tip-actioned match rods, an all-through action general purpose rod is better for coping with weed. Hooks should match the size of bait being used, but it is always wise to err on the large side for tench are rarely hook-shy and the bigger the hook the better the hold. In fact, I wouldn't hesitate to use a size 12, even if using maggots, and a size 10 is not too large for a thumb-nail-sized lump of bread-flake.

Floatfishing, with the bait laid hard on the bottom, is by far the best method for canal tench. No special floats are necessary but they should be kept as small as possible to lessen resistance when the bait is taken. How the terminal tackle is set up depends really on the type of bottom. Normally the lead shot is best placed in a bunch down towards the hook. This will give an immediate signal when the bait is taken. In weedy swims, however, the lead shot would drag the bait out of sight in which case it pays to keep the bulk shot above the weed with perhaps one 'tell tale' dust shot, say a foot from the hook.

The problem of what bait to use also crops up in weedy swims. Maggots or casters, and worms, soon get hidden in blanket weed, therefore breadflake or crust, which sink slowly, would be far better. When a tench takes the bait the signal is usually quite positive and the float sails away out of sight. But, because of the way in which they feed (with their heads down and their tails up) they are apt to knock the line, thus registering false bites. In fact these are known as 'line bites' and can be troublesome at times. One way of avoiding this situation is to have a very long tail between the hook and the first shot.

Another way is to use the 'lift' method. The idea behind this is to have just one heavy shot attached very close to the hook so that when the fish picks up the bait it also lifts the shot. The shot should be heavy enough to pull the float right

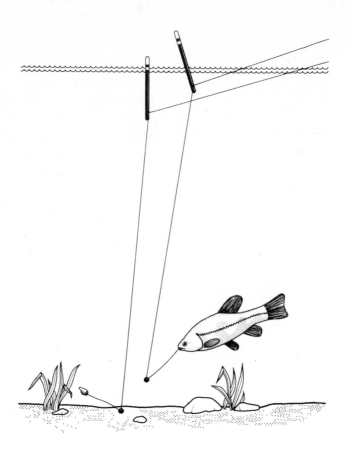

Fig 6 The lift method is a popular technique for summer tench fishing. When the fish picks up the bait it also lifts the shot. When the weight of the shot is displaced the float rises out of the water giving an unmistakable indication of a bite

down to the merest tip in the water and placed at the exact depth, about an inch from the hook. The float should be fastened by the bottom ring only and held in place with a rubber band or by passing the line through the ring two or three times. It is a sensitive method that gives a clear bite signal – the float rises like a submarine periscope when the fish picks up the bait and the shot.

6 Match Fishing

Canals have always been closely associated with match fishing, which is hardly surprising because the popular sport more or less began on Northern waterways. Records are in existence of contests in Lancashire and Yorkshire as early as the 1850s. True, they were only small affairs among groups of mill workers and miners, who threw a few pence into a kitty to add a touch of excitement to otherwise mediocre fishing. Nevertheless it was a start, and by the end of the century Yorkshire and Lancashire anglers had perfected match techniques and methods that are still used today.

For instance, 19th century canal fishermen knew all about colouring maggots, and used squatts, pinkies and sour milk maggots as well as bloodworms, so little has changed in the last hundred years. Of course the tackle in those days was quite crude and nowhere near fine enough to attract fish in any quantity. But despite the handicap of horsehair or catgut hooklengths and silk lines, those early pioneers were obviously on the right track.

Canals are now regarded as ideal training grounds for match fishing on all types of water and it is no coincidence that many of our top flight matchmen began their careers along the towpaths. These household names readily admit that the experience gained catching shy fish from narrow canals stands them in good stead on all other waters, especially when the going is hard.

International Tony Scott from Burton-on-Trent is a prime example. Tony spent many years specialising in canal match fishing in the Midlands before turning his attention to larger and more variable waters further afield. He is convinced that the lessons he learned while canal fishing help him at all hard-fished venues. Tony reckons that the use of fine tackle and ways of tempting nervous fish are now second nature to him.

In extolling the virtues of canals as match fishing nurseries, I need only mention that living legend Benny Ashurst. Benny, who must rank as one of the greatest match anglers the country has produced, began his career on the Lancashire 'cuts'. In the 1950s he earned the title 'King of the Canals' with hundreds of victories. The methods he evolved, particularly with casters and stick floats (he was the first man to exploit casters and he invented the stick float) proved deadly wherever he went and, over 20 years later, they are still unbeatable.

So what is special about canal match fishing? In a nutshell it means catching fish under some of the most difficult conditions possible. The top-class canal match angler is skilled in the art of tempting educated and finicky fish from clear, shallow, water within the confines of a narrow, ten-yard-long swim, usually devoid of any bankside cover, while surrounded by other anglers. Add to this the fact that most contests take place in the middle of the day when the fish are generally

The Grand Union Canal at Rowington, near Warwick. A popular winter venue for matchman and pleasure angler

somewhat lethargic, and you can see how difficult it must be. To catch even a few ounces in such a situation demands the utmost patience and know-how plus extremely fine tackle and the best bait available.

It is not always as bad as I have described; often the canal is coloured and has a reasonable depth and width plus a large head of small fish, but, overall, the canal matchman could hardly be more handicapped as the result sheets generally show. Ounces are sometimes enough to win big contests and five pounds is regarded as an excellent weight on the majority of waterways. Such results hardly indicate the amount of effort and preparation that goes into a match. So why do men bother? What's the attraction? Well, there are several reasons, not the least being that in some areas of the country canals are the only waters available within a reasonable distance. In places where other, much better quality fishing can be had, such as the Midlands, the answer lies in the evenness of canal fishing and the comparatively low cost.

All too often along river match lengths, it's the peg rather than the angler that wins matches. Of course, this may apply at some canal venues too, but to nowhere near the same extent. As international Ken Giles put it 'Canals are among the few remaining venues where skill and experience alone win matches.' This is particularly true of the West Midlands where, in recent years, comparative novices, using swim-feeders, have claimed victory at big events on the Rivers Severn and Avon. While the fact that mere beginners can beat seasoned experts is good for the sport in that it encourages new blood, it's a trend that has turned many major river matches into little more than a lottery. Hence the growing popularity of canal contests in which luck plays a much lesser part.

The growing expense of river fishing is also an important factor. While it can cost at least £5 for enough bait to stand any chance at all on rivers, many big canal matches have been won with a slice of bread. Yet the prize money can be just as valuable. Hinckley match ace Billy Makin can confirm this. His winnings, mostly from canal events, totalled a fantastic £6000 in the 1978/79 season. True, £2000 came from a national competition and £2000 off the bookies, but the fact remains that Bill's prowess on the towpaths was the main contributing factor. Bill reckons his bait, apart from the occasions when he is forced to buy bloodworms and jokers, costs him around 50p a week – not bad considering his returns. But then he breeds all his own hook maggots during summer and autumn and also collects a lot of bloodworms and jokers.

Compare this with the half gallons, or even gallons, of maggots plus the same amount of casters and all the other alternatives essential for most river matches and it becomes clear why many anglers are turning to canal contests.

Basic Match Tackle

Small to medium-sized roach and gudgeon are the match angler's usual quarry, though skimmer bream and tiny carp are now turning up more and more along many waterways. Larger fish, such as tench, bream, carp, perch and occasional chub, also play a part on some canals and when present often determine the basic tackle rigs.

If gudgeon were the prime target, and this applies on many match lengths, a short pole, say the top three joints, is sometimes the only rod necessary. Scores of matches on the Shropshire Union, Staffs–Worcester, Trent and Mersey and Grand Union, to name but a few, are won fishing close in with a short pole. But pre-knowledge of the course is obviously vital before such a choice is made.

At venues where better-class fish are caught, a 12 or 13-foot rod, either with a centre pin or fixed spool reel, would be first choice, with a long or short pole set up just in case. There again, at venues where bream are the normal match winners, as on certain Northern and Southern canals, a short leger rod with a swing or quiver tip would be the main rig.

As I have already stated it is essential to do some homework beforehand about the type of fish likely to be encountered because the three-hour duration of the majority of canal matches leaves little time for experiment. But if in doubt, set up float rod, poles and leger rigs, and play it by ear.

Lines are normally kept as fine as possible, again depending on the canal, but generally 1½lb breaking strain reel line, together with 1lb breaking strain hook lengths, are pretty standard and fine enough for all but the most frequented venues. The latter often demand 1lb reel line and 12 or 10oz bottoms to make an impression.

Pole tackles are made up beforehand with floats, shots and hooks assembled and wound on line wrappers. These lines are measured accurately for various permutations of pole lengths so that hooked fish swing comfortably to hand when the pole is held vertically. They are easily and quickly attached to the pole by two or three pieces of rubber tubing or to a short length of elastic permanently fastened to the pole tip.

Although the elastic helps absorb the shock of hooking and lifting fish and so minimizes smashes, it is not really essential for canal fishing. In any case, if there are good sample fish around, a float rod and reel is a much better proposition. To save valuable time many match anglers whip one or two small rings to the second top joints of their poles and use them as an aid to shortening or lengthening the line. In practice they tie a loop in the end of the line, pass this through the rubber tube fasteners and wrap the line round one of the rings until it is the required length before pushing the rubbers into place on the tip.

Floats need to be ultra-sensitive for match fishing and, besides those described under general canal tackle, there are several varieties, often home made, used by leading names. Worth mentioning are loaded balsa antennae for normal conditions and loaded crow quill, which gives the little extra buoyancy needed in rough water. The balsa antenna is carved in one piece from ⅜in balsa dowel of a hard grade which, besides being tough, has very little buoyancy. The overall length is six inches and only the size of the body is varied. This can be lengthened to carry a little extra lead to help longer casting. The stem of the float is gradually tapered from the tip, which is left at ¹⁄₁₆in thick. This makes it extremely sensitive and one No. 8 dust shot is enough to pull it down one and a half inches. In fact, these floats are so sensitive that it is necessary to set up the tackle and adjust the shot beforehand because it takes far too long during a match.

After being fashioned, the floats are loaded with lead wire so that when three No. 8 shot are attached the tip protrudes about 1/16in above the surface. Two of these shot are used to lock the float in position and the other to sink the bait and complete the trimming of the float. The best way to load the float is to whip a wire ring to the base and then attach a small swivel. The lead wire can then be wrapped around the swivel and glued with epoxy resin into place. The three dust shot should be fastened to the float during the operation and the float tested on a canal to gauge the correct amount of wire needed. This is to take into account the weight of sunken line. The body and stem should then be varnished or painted to make watertight and the tip painted in your favourite colour.

The crow quills, which need to be as straight as possible, are useful when there is a ripple or swell on the surface and should receive the same treatment except that a No. 4 shot is added to the three dust and also a fraction more tip left showing.

Since pole fishing became popular Continental type floats have proved their worth for close in and middle canal fishing. Patterns made from balsa with nylon bristle tips and sometimes wire stems are ideal when conditions are good. But these floats are extremely sensitive and difficult to trim. Micro dust shot are often necessary to get the correct amount of tip showing, which is another reason why pole tackles are made up in advance.

Fine wire, blued or gilt spade ends in sizes from 18 to 24 are the most widely used hooks, and they are normally tied to 18 inch or two foot hook lengths of 1lb (or less) breaking strain. A supply tied to 1½lb breaking strain line may be necessary if large fish can be expected but, generally speaking, it would be fatal to use hooks larger than size 18, or thicker hook lengths than 1½lb. There are always exceptions, obviously, but a study of match results throughout the country indicates that most contests are won on size 20s tied to 1lb bottoms, and this applies even when bream are involved.

Some experts prefer barbless hooks for bloodworm fishing because these make it much easier to hook this fragile bait. But there is no need to buy barbless patterns: just break off the barb with a pair of pliers. As most baits sink naturally under their own weight and quite fast enough in shallow water very little shot is required – just enough to trim the float and help overcome wind problems. For this reason shotting can be reduced to a simple formula, providing the float is preloaded.

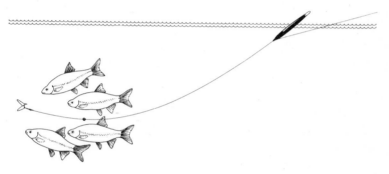

Fig 7 Lightly shotted self-cocking floats can be used to good advantage when the fish are feeding ravenously near the surface of the canal. A single small shot is all that is needed between float and hook to prevent tangles

The most sensitive set-up is to have just one dust shot between the float and the hook. The shot can be adjusted for maximum bite registration depending on how the fish are feeding. For instance, if gudgeon are feeding you will want to get the bait down as quickly as possible, so the shot can be placed within an inch or two of the hook. The same applies if roach are taking 'on the drop'. In these circumstances, the nearer the shot is to the hook the sooner you will notice that the bait has stopped falling.

On the other hand, if the fish are finicky and shy it may be necessary to place the shot well away from the hook so that it doesn't affect the way the bait falls. In this respect it should be remembered that the hook length can affect the speed at which the bait sinks: it usually slows it up. This is why a micro dust shot on the hook length sometimes helps to bring more bites, simply because it counteracts the buoyancy of the nylon line.

In rough weather an extra shot is often necessary in order to present a natural bait and to keep the float stable and this is when the crow quill can be used. This float, fished over depth, is also useful when there is a strong pull on the canal: a shot can be fastened to the hook length to help prevent the bait being dragged along too quickly by the faster moving surface water.

The basic baits for modern canal match fishing are maggots, small gozzers, pinkies, squatts and sour milk specials, casters, bloodworms and punched bread. Other baits sometimes score, depending on the canal, but generally it pays to stick to the well-proven basics. How and when they are used will be dependent on the colour of the canal, the size, quantity and species of fish, and the time of the year, etc. For instance, maggots suspended in very cold water often tighten up and become lifeless, in which case punched bread or casters often prove a more tempting bait.

On the other hand in summer, if the canal is very coloured (as it often is when there is a lot of boat traffic) wriggling maggots or bloodworms are much more likely to attract fish. Match anglers mostly use very fine brown breadcrumb or biscuit meal groundbait and mix it as lightly as possible to form a non-feeding cloud. Very small finger-nail-sized pieces are thrown into the swim at regular intervals according to how the fish are feeding and, if maggots are being used as hookbait, they sometimes add a pinch of squatts to every piece.

Techniques and Methods. . . . Preparation

Several factors influence match tactics, the most important being the colour of the water – clear or cloudy. The number and species of fish likely to be caught should also be taken into account and an estimate made of a weight to aim for.

Weather conditions will probably dictate tackle rigs, especially if it is windy when a lot of consideration will have to be given to counteracting surface drift or drag. Boat traffic will also play a big part in determining methods because often in summer the procession is endless.

Generally speaking, the majority of our canals carry a lot of pleasure craft and are permanently coloured throughout the summer months, and they usually remain 'soupy' until the boat traffic ceases around October time. The reason for this is that the water is never allowed to settle for a long enough period for the sediment and mud to clear. Even first thing in the morning, when there hasn't been a boat through for several hours, much of the silt stirred up the previous day remains suspended.

Algae, of course, also add colour on many canals, but the green tinge created by the myriads of minute plants on which fish feed is a completely different proposition. Actually I always feel much more confident of catching fish when there are a lot of algae in the water. As far as I'm concerned this growth is a sure sign of reasonable water quality and it seems to suggest that fish are present. One of the most noticeable things I remember about the canals struck by the fish disease of the middle sixties was the clarity of the water. Not only had the fish disappeared but also all the algae. The transition was sudden and heartbreaking and there has never been a satisfactory explanation to my mind.

On the Trent and Mersey Canal, for instance, we found ourselves struggling for bites on a stretch that had been absolutely alive with fish of all species the previous season but which was now gin clear. The last match I fished there for a number of years, in 1967, still sticks in my mind, as the entry of 70 good canal anglers failed to raise so much as a bite, yet the year before 2lb wouldn't have made the prize list. But that is now history and thankfully that particular stretch at King's Bromley is again fishing quite well.

But to get back to tactics. On coloured canals, fish can often be caught quite close in, which is an obvious place to begin, especially if a lot of boats can be expected. And remember that though all may appear peaceful when the match commences early in the morning, that inviting far side may become inaccessible within a short time of the cavalcade of boats.

If you have done your homework, and no serious match angler would dream of fishing a strange venue without finding out in advance what fish he is likely to catch and the best bait for the job, you will have formed some sort of plan. This may seem a tall task to the beginner but it is not all that difficult. Match reports in the angling press are always worth studying and noting, as they invariably indicate what the winner caught, together with baits and methods used. But don't take it all as gospel truth: many top names are reluctant to reveal their secrets and are apt to be rather deceptive where reporters are concerned. I should know, I have interviewed enough of these types in my time, so try to read between the lines.

Another source of information is the match organiser. If he can't put you right himself he will probably know someone willing to help. Big names in match fishing never have any problems in this respect for they help each other to a surprising degree.

The NFA's Team Knock Out competition is a good example of how anglers get up-to-the-minute information on strange venues. Being closely involved with many West Midland squads I can tell you it doesn't take them long to build up a complete dossier on any unfamiliar water.

So, presuming you now have the necessary information, let's assume the match takes place in summer along a length that holds a fair head of gudgeon, some roach, plus occasional bream and other larger species. It's a situation typical of many canals these days and I have chosen it to illustrate the different baits, tackle rigs, methods etc. that could come up trumps. That's the beauty of canal fishing: there are so many alternatives it never gets boring. Of course, many match anglers, particularly from Lancashire, are prepared to pin their faith in one method or bait wherever they go. Some fish casters across the far bank, others use only bloodworms no matter what the venue.

These anglers do well providing they choose their matches carefully, and I admire them, but I have more respect for the anglers who are prepared to experiment and fish anywhere. It's been said that more canal matches are won in the garden shed or garage than on the waterside and there's a lot of truth in this. Preparation is the key to success, without it you are wasting your time, and it can begin as long as three weeks before each match with maggot breeding or bloodworm collecting. But the actual spade work for each event is done the previous night or early on the morning. So let's take a look at what's involved, first with the bait department.

As the canal we are fishing has a large head of small to medium sized fish, maggots are our first choice and we have several different types (gozzers, pinkies, squatts and sour brans) in various shades and colours, plus maybe a few ordinary commercials. These will have been stored in a fridge or cool place after being removed from the feed as late as possible.

There are many arguments on how fresh a bait should be, many matchmen preferring absolutely fresh maggots so full of feed that they are almost black in appearance, maintaining that the fresher the maggot the more soft and lively it is. In fact I know men who take the pigeon, heart or whatever, with them to the match and pick their hook maggots straight from the meat, and they certainly can't come any fresher than that.

On the other hand, there are the anglers who prefer well-scoured baits and wash their maggots under luke-warm water before placing them in damp bran or breadcrumbs for a final polish. The answer, I suppose, is to experiment until you are satisfied either way. Personally I have never been able to prove the argument and, as I like a snack while fishing, I plump for the cleaned maggots.

Like most home breeders I remove them from the feed the day or evening before a match, riddle off any rubbish and store them in dampened bran. This gives me time to colour them if I think it is necessary. The same routine applies to any maggots that have to be purchased from tackle dealers.

Few anglers bother to breed squatts, and as these are delivered to and stored and sold by the tackleists in sand, it's a good idea to clean them if only to see if you've got your money's worth. The sand is easily removed through a sieve or a fine riddle and then the squatts can be washed in lukewarm or cold water and dried off in fine breadcrumbs or groundbait.

A word of warning here: never fridge squatts for more than a few days as they soon die in cold temperatures, and even when they appear to be in good condition squatts that have been in a fridge for any length of time tend to float. While preparing squatts always pick out a few of the bigger ones for the hook. They can prove a good alternative when sport is slow.

Having sorted our maggots, casters are the next item and though they are by no means the great match winners they once were few match anglers would dream of going to a match without any. You don't need a great amount for a three-hour canal contest: half a pint is ample, so there is no problem in preparing your own. How to do this is described in the chapter on baits. As top quality casters can be obtained from most tackle shops this is one job that could be dispensed with but, as with maggots, the majority of matchmen prefer to do this task themselves.

This might be a good time to re-assure anyone who is not in a position to breed his own maggots that matches are won with commercially obtained baits. In fact there is little option from October onwards when artificial heating of some kind is necessary for breeding. There are anglers who have heated fly-houses who are able to breed maggots all the year round, but they are few and far between.

Returning to casters, however, these are normally regarded as a by-product of large maggots, but the chrysalids of pinkies, squatts and sour brans should not be neglected. Although much smaller they are no less effective in tempting fish; indeed they can on occasions prove more attractive. I have caught lots of roach and bream with the tiny chrysalids of the squatt.

Hempseed is the next item (provided it is allowed: it is still barred on some waters) and, while hemp is rarely used these days as a hook bait in matches, it is always a good alternative. A little mixed in with the groundbait or loose feed does no harm either, and it helps to keep the fish in the swim. In the Midlands hempseed is considered an essential ingredient of all feed, particularly when casters are being used on the hook.

Because the canal is likely to be coloured, bread in any form is hardly likely to be of much use, so we can forget it. But if there is the slightest chance of the water being clear, such as a disused canal free of boats, it could be the first item to be stowed in the basket. However, this is discussed under clear-water conditions.

Recapping, we have our maggots and casters, plus a little hempseed, so what else might be needed? A few small red worms may come in handy if perch and small pike happen to put in an appearance, which happens frequently on some canals. Bream are not averse to a wriggling worm either, so if it is not too much trouble make a habit of carrying a few worms to every match. That then is our regular bait supply, apart from bloodworms and jokers, which I have purposely left until last. This is because bloodworms are still banned in many matches and also it is a bait that usually only scores when the going is hard and ounces can win the match. Lanca-shire anglers who specialise in fishing the 'little red men', as bloodworms are called, would perhaps argue with this state-ment but, in considering the country's canals as a whole I feel it is true. It certainly applies in my own neck of the woods, the West Midlands.

Most Midland canal match anglers use bloodworms and jokers but they invariably try maggots or casters first. One of the reasons for this is that 'bloods' are snapped up by stickle-backs which can waste a lot of time. On the other hand a good dodge and one that often works is to feed jokers (rules permitting) and offer maggots or casters on the hook, thus getting the best of both worlds. For this exercise we will take jokers and 'bloods' along just in case. The bloodworms can be left in the newspaper wrapping used to store them and packed in the basket or bait bag, but the jokers need to be mixed in more dampened peat ready for feeding. Some anglers prefer to do this at the waterside in the same manner as we add squatts to groundbait. This way the amount of real bait being introduced can be carefully monitored. Incidentally, a little fine foundry sand or soil mixed in with the peat ensures the balls or small pieces of feed sink quickly.

Having taken care of the bait supply the next job is mixing the groundbait. The quantity will depend on the species of fish population of the match length. In our case bream can be expected in some areas so we may require a fair amount, say four pints of dry fine breadcrumb. For emergencies we can take a reserve supply in its dry state and mix it during the match. The crumb or biscuit meal will already have been sieved to remove any lumps so all that is required is to add water.

Always mix groundbait in a large shallow bowl and add water a little at a time while constantly rubbing the crumb between the hands. Aim for a mixture that just about clings together when lightly squeezed. Mixed this way the ground-bait falls lightly on the water with very little splash and it breaks up into an attractive non-feeding cloud as it falls to the bottom. If you want it to sink to the bottom before breaking up, add more water, or better still a little sand. If prepared the previous night the mixture will tend to dry out unless it is covered with a wet cloth or stored in an airtight polythene bag, but before doing this run the groundbait through a fine riddle to remove any lumps.

Finally on the subject of groundbait I must mention the malt dust mixture which was once so popular with South Staffordshire anglers. If you can get hold of some malt dust prepare it as described elsewhere and give it a try. As far as I'm concerned malt dust is the best non-feeding mixture of all. What's more its brown colour should appeal to matchmen who dislike a white 'carpet' on the canal bottom.

With bait and tackle ready all we now require is a good draw but this is something we can do nothing about. I said earlier that in general canal matches offer the majority of entries a fair crack of the whip but there are always better lengths than others. However, over a period luck has a habit of sharing itself out so it's a case of always being fully prepared for when your chance comes.

Having arrived at our peg the first thing to note is the colour of the water, the direction of the pull or flow if any, and whether there are any natural or artificial features that may offer some advantage. Although most canals are featureless and uniform there are sometimes streams or ditches running in, pipes discharging effluent from sewage works or factories, cow drinks on the opposite bank etc. that may attract fish to the vicinity. Weedbeds on the near or far banks always help as they provide useful cover, but all too often there is little to distinguish one peg from another.

Assembling tackle is the next job and if possible, as I have stressed elsewhere, should be done well away from the waterside. Remember that the fish are nervous enough without the scaring vibrations created by anglers tramping along the towpath. And never stand close to the water's edge even if the water happens to look like Brown Windsor soup. Keep a low profile at all times.

Set up a pole, float rod and swing or quiver tip outfit complete to hook and place them within handy reach. Basket or box should be set in a position as far back from the water's edge as we can fish comfortably and at a slight angle so that we sit looking downstream or towards the pull. Actually, the more you have to lean forward the better as this helps in achieving that low profile. The rest of the tackle, accessories etc. and bait should be placed so that it is all immediately to hand yet out of the way.

While tackling up and waiting to begin, a plan of action should be worked out. For instance, if there is a good head of gudgeon and small roach (and we have already established that there is) we can start by fishing for these close in with a short pole and later switch to the far bank with casters for the better class roach or maybe the near side of the far shelf for the bream, bearing in mind that the near and far shelves are usually more productive in summer than the boat channel.

For gudgeon and small roach the short pole (the top three joints of the normal 18-footer) is ready with a swan shot pinched to the hook to ascertain the exact depth. Before the starting signal has died away the float should be in the water and an accurate assessment of the depth made from the middle (or as far as the pole will reach) to the near bank.

To begin fishing we'll choose a spot slightly downstream, say three or four yards out, and set the float so that the hook bait just touches bottom. A single pinkie on a size 20 hook is as good as anything for openers. To attract the fish we'll feed squatts in small pieces of groundbait. Three walnut-sized balls placed precisely in a space about a foot square are enough at this stage with a few loose pinkies in exactly the same spot. A dozen or so casters catapulted or thrown to the far side should also be injected at this stage.

If we are lucky bites will come almost immediately and the next step is to speed up the catch rate. For gudgeon this can be done by gradually feeding closer, always remembering that you need at least 15 inches of water as cover. We could also switch to a float that carries a fair sized shot, say 1AAA, to get the bait down through the first 12 inches of water very quickly. Such a float should be set with the main shot 12 inches below it and a dust shot halfway between the AAA and the hook.

If fish are coming freely, and three a minute is not imposs-ible in the early stages along the better canals, we need to feed regularly but as sparsely as possible. Feeding is probably the most important factor in ensuring you make the most of your opportunities, but it can only be learned by experience. The line between just enough and too much is a very narrow one, yet overstep it and you'll kill the swim. Generally though it is always good practice to underfeed.

If gudgeon are coming fast we can try a large commercial maggot because gudgeon are not too fussy in summer and if it is accepted we can really go to town and save re-baiting for several gudgeon can be caught on the same maggot even when it is in shreds. In this situation, when the shoal is really feeding in earnest they will take practically any old maggot.

They will also give away their exact position by a stream of bubbles erupting on the surface so you can drop the bait in the centre of the shoal every time.

At times like this we should be able to compile quite a useful weight, say three hundred fish in three hours. If that seems a lot I should explain that the picture in my mind is the Staffs–Worcester Canal where gudgeon run 45 to the pound, so it works out under 4lb. If the small roach are dominant we can speed up by encouraging them to take 'on the drop'. We do this by regularly feeding cloud and squatts, keeping the groundbait to thumbnail-sized pieces and not trying to bring them in close. Also, we'll keep flicking the rod tip to keep the bait moving.

If bites start to fade it calls for a change from pinkies to sour brans and if they refuse these a couple of squatts, or a pinkie or squatt chrysalis. So far so good, but now let's look at a more likely situation when the match does not go to plan.

It may be that we can't get a bite from the initial spot, or that fish come far too slowly. If we stick to more or less the same area the first thing that's called for is a smaller hook – either a 22 or 24. It's amazing how often this works but supposing it doesn't, we'll have to try a different bait, but unless the match is going to be won with ounces it's hardly worth trying sour brans for gudgeon. After permutating baits in several different spots between the middle and close in without success, a change of tactics is called for.

As we failed to find gudgeon or small roach in quantity on the near shelf, the chances are that there are none on the far side either but we can give it a quick try with a full length pole, before switching to float rod and reel with casters in search of better-class fish. For this style the caster needs to be presented reasonably stationary on the far shelf a foot or so from the bank with as little lead as possible beneath the float. There may be only 12 inches of water on the far scour but this doesn't matter if the water is coloured. In any case, fish are far less nervous when tucked away under the far bank.

We'll start with a size 18 long-shanked hook buried completely inside the caster. Leave the hook visible and nine times

out of ten you will be 'shelled': that is the roach will suck the
fluid from inside the caster and leave the husk on the hook.
Set it about six inches over depth and place the shot to hang
just off bottom. Cast as near the far bank as possible and bury
the line underwater immediately to prevent drag. If the fish
are right under the bank we can't afford to pull on the float
while sinking the line so we must make the line sink naturally
under its own weight. A quick way of doing this is to take a
small ball of mud between thumb and forefinger and pull the
line through it while reeling in. Some anglers carry fuller's
earth especially for this purpose.

Another way is to use back shot above the float but you will
need a different pattern for this. Peacock quill wagglers, with
or without an inserted tip, are ideal for far bank fishing, particularly in windy weather. Their advantage is that the line can
be sunk quite deep with back shotting. Patterns about five or
six inches long are most suitable and are locked on the line
with a couple of good sized shot. Any other lead required to
'dot' a waggler right down to the surface, other than the back
shot and a couple of dust shot towards the hook, should also
be placed at the base of the float.

If Lady Luck is with us those casters thrown across at the
start will have got the roach interested and we may not have
to wait long for a bite. Anyway, give it about ten minutes
before introducing more, then throw in half a dozen or so
every ten minutes. The float at this stage is just about visible
and virtually still just under the far bank, and that's where we
need to keep it. It's not easy if the canal is pulling or it's
windy, but more about that later.

We are concentrating hard, our reflexes ready to strike at
any unusual movement of the float. Certainly it's no good
waiting for it to disappear. Remember we have six inches of
hook length on the bottom and it's surprising what fish can do
to a bait without giving away their presence even when it is
suspended in mid water.

The reason we are overdepth, by the way, is because the
swim is so shallow. We could trip bottom which is a far more
sensitive rig, but with only 12 or so inches of water available it

would invariably lead to tangles when casting or striking. On some canals the far shelf is the deepest part and with 18 inches or more, obviously we would commence 'tripping'.

Let's assume that the float moves. We strike and meet resistance. Now, casters nearly always attract a good stamp of fish so it could be a roach of anything up to half a pound or more. If it is a good one don't give it time to panic and scare away any others in the swim but drag it firmly but gently towards the middle with the follow through action of the strike. Fish often come easily at this moment. Then, if it is spirited, it can be played out in deeper water where it can do no harm.

Don't worry if bites stop coming for a time as this method calls for patience. Just contemplate the fact that half a dozen good roach may be enough to win, and above all don't increase the rate of feeding. It's all too easy to keep feeding when there's nothing happening if only to break the monotony, but it can be fatal.

If the first target point fails to produce we can twitch or drag the hook bait gradually off the shelf, allowing it to remain still for a while at different points as we cover the area where casters fell short. We do this by lifting the rod gently. After 30 minutes if nothing happens it's time for another change of tactics.

Here I think I should mention the importance of having confidence in your methods. Confidence, in fact, is one of the main ingredients in a successful match angler's outlook. It is certainly necessary for far-side caster fishing. Many top names use this method exclusively if they know a canal holds roach. They stick it out patiently, sometimes waiting an hour or so for a bite and then come out on top. Furthermore they leave the bait as long as 15 minutes before re-casting. So, are there roach about or not? A good way of finding out is to pull the float up and lay hard on – three or four feet if necessary. Bites are not easy to detect with this style but if fish are around they rarely refuse such a presentation of hook bait.

It may well be that our first method didn't hold the bait still enough, so we'll give it a try. Obviously, shotting will have to be altered so, for a start, raise the bottom shot so that it is still suspended, and fish a long tail. If the canal is pulling we can add two or three more dust shot on the line lying on the bottom to further anchor the bait. We place these at intervals with the first about eight inches from the hook. Laying hard on is as good a method there is for all baits and for most species when fish are hard to come by.

If this style doesn't produce after half an hour it could be time for another change, depending on the grapevine or what's happening around us. On most canals it's possible to watch the opposition for long distances on each side of your peg so we should have a fair idea of what is going on. If nothing is being caught it might pay us to stay across the far side, but it's always worthwhile going back on the pole to the baited near side pitch for a short spell at intervals.

If it's a really bad day we could stick with the bloodworm close in or even try it across with the float rod. Feeding jokers in 'black' little and often, and offering one, two or even three 'bloods' on a 20 or 22 hook is a deadly method on hammered canals. When most, or all, entries use 'bloods' many make it a rule to feed jokers raw, having stored them this way after collecting. I have never tried it myself for the simple reason I have never been able to collect enough to do this, but the method is reputed to give that little extra edge.

In trying to describe the various tactics used in match fishing it is difficult to lay down any hard and fast rules because all methods and tackle rigs, as well as baits, can be permutated to some extent. For instance we could lay on close in, or in the boat channel, with casters or even bloodworms. We could trip the far shelf with chrysoidined pinkies, or perhaps a couple of squatts, or a squatt and a squatt chrysalis cocktail. The list is endless and anything is worth trying when the fish won't respond.

At this point I should like to go back to the start of the match, to a peg in an area known to hold bream – skimmers and bigger fish. Here, bream would obviously be uppermost in our minds so we would lay plans accordingly and bait up a selected spot at the start, as we did with casters for the roach.

Because bream like plenty of water on their backs a likely point is just beyond middle on the edge of the far shelf, so we put in two or three golf-ball-sized lumps of groundbait, well laced with squatts plus the hempseed already mixed in. An initial ten-minute session laying on with a pole or float rod offering a gozzer or a couple of pinkies on a size 20, should determine whether we are in luck. If not (as usually happens) we can go in search of small stuff as we did at the other peg, returning at intervals for another try. But, if bream are taken at other pegs in the vicinity, it would pay us to stay there and wait our turn for bream frequently move up and down lengths of canal. At one or two canal venues bream always figure in the leading catches and matchmen set out their stalls accordingly, ignoring any other fish and playing the waiting game just as others do for roach with casters.

A favourite rig for this style is a light leger (one or two swan-shot link) with sour bran maggots, squatts or pinkies, and a quiver or swing tip rod to present the tackle well across in an area carpeted with squatts and groundbait. Very small bream, two or three-ounce fish, are quite common in some canals and they usually respond well to float tactics, frequently taking on the drop as do small roach. When this happens the single dust shot antenna works very efficiently especially if the shot is placed close to the hook.

So far I have covered most popular methods that work when conditions allow, but all too often we are handicapped by weather, or boats, and so must adjust according to circumstances. One of the most frustrating situations is when the canal flows first one way and then the other as locks are emptied or filled. Depending on how close we are to the lock the current can be quite considerable, sometimes faster than a river in spate, and when this happens the only solution is to float leger reasonably close in.

A good rig here, and one that also helps to beat the wind, is a float fastened top and bottom, or double rubber, anchored with a swan shot link leger. Set the float overdepth to lay flat and it will cock as it is pulled around by the flow pushing against the line. The reel, or pole, line should of course be

held tight. Float legering close in is also quite often the only
way to fish when boat traffic is very heavy. On canals where
there is always a steady flow, such as the Taunton–
Bridgwater, a small stick float is ideal for trotting through the
swim.

October is an important month on the canal match angler's
calendar for it marks the end of the holiday season when most
boats are moored up for the winter. Now the canals are peaceful and gradually clear until frosts complete the transforma-
tion by killing off the algae and weed growth. The
temperature of the water also drops which means fish may
seek the deeper water in the boat channel. They will also be
less active and therefore a little more difficult to tempt. This
doesn't necessarily mean that sport is slower than in summer.
On the contrary, providing the weather is reasonably mild
excellent bags can be taken especially in October and Novem-
ber.

Clear water means changes in match tactics, mainly in the
spots we fish and in baits. For a start we can forget close-in
techniques unless there is an abnormal depth of water. The
area we concentrate on now is the boat channel or the far
shelf. But first, let's consider our bait requirements.

Bread is one of the first items on the list and, as the punch is
an excellent method of using it, we want a few slices of really
fresh bread. Stale bread is useless because it won't stay on the
hook. Toasters or thick sliced loaves are the best.

Casters are just as effective in winter as they are in summer
so we need about half a pint. For maggots we have to rely on
the tackle shops so we are limited to pinkies, squatts and large
commercials. Nevertheless we can colour them if required
and in this respect chrysoidined maggots of all types are
beginning to score on canals as they have on all other waters.
In addition we will carry bloodworms and jokers, providing
they are allowed. Very little groundbait is necessary, less than
half the quantity we use in summer, and for punch fishing
some of this can be mixed quite sloppy unless cloud is preferred.

We begin with the punch and tackle up with a loaded balsa

antenna (wind allowing) fastening it on the line to suspend the bait just off bottom midway between middle and far bank. Place the single dust shot about six inches from a size 20 hook for we shall probably get a lot of 'drop' bites. Impale a bread pellet from the smallest size punch on the hook and we're ready to start. One small piece of groundbait or a few bread pellets previously punched out is usually enough to ensure immediate results and this should be thrown in the target area slightly to our left or right depending on the pull.

Remember it is always better to fish in the direction of the flow rather than directly in front, mainly because you can manipulate the tackle more easily when it is at an angle. The great thing about the bread punch, which applies equally as well to small pieces of flake, is that it brings bites very quickly. In fact, if we don't get a bite in the first ten minutes, and after trying other spots, we might as well forget it. If small roach and bream are around they rarely refuse bread, but unfortunately they soon lose interest, particularly in matches, although of course there are the odd exceptions.

Anyway, if we do begin catching we can introduce a little more feed and perhaps try a larger pellet to attract better class fish. While fishing the punch it pays to keep the bait on the move by flicking the rod and raising the float, but do it gently or you could dislodge the bread from the hook. When the bites stop coming regularly it's not a bad idea to try casting a little farther over and slightly downstream as the shoal tend to move with the flow.

If this doesn't do the trick it's time for a change and now we can try casters, maggots or bloodworms in the boat channel or well across. Bloodworms and jokers are a fine combination in winter and, what's more, there is no need to restrict feeding quite so much as with other baits. Often when the weather is cold bloodworms fished with conventional float tackle rather than a pole will attract class fish. Casters, too, score heavily in clear water and they can be tripped down the boat channel or the far shelf, or layed hard on when sport is slow. Feed sparingly when the weather is cold and don't expect firm bites.

Frequently, when laying on, the only indication that a fish

has picked up the caster is a slight trembling of the float tip. Watch carefully for such signals and strike at the merest flicker. A single chrysoidine or bronze maggot offered well on bottom and twitched from the far shelf to the middle is another good method that has won a few winter events in the Midlands, but in cold water the bait needs changing frequently as the maggots soon become lifeless.

7 Where to Fish

THE MAJOR CANALS – NORTH

Bridgewater Canal

The first lengthy canal (28½ miles in all) to be opened in this country, the Bridgewater is also unique in being one of the few privately owned waterways, the owners being the Manchester Ship Canal Company. It runs from Castlefield, Manchester, at the junction of the Rochdale Canal to join the Trent and Mersey Canal at Preston Brook and then on to the River Mersey at Runcorn. From Manchester the Stretford and Leigh Branch extends for 11 miles to the Leeds and Liverpool Canal at Leigh. Another unusual feature of the Bridgewater is that it has no locks, except at Runcorn where ten were constructed to take it down to the River Mersey.

An important north-west match venue, the Bridgewater Canal has a chequered history as a fishery with good years interspersed with bad. Although some sections have fished reasonably well in recent years, other previously good lengths have yielded very little. Local anglers blame an abundance of natural food, including bloodworms, in many stretches as the reason why the fish refuse their baits. An instance of this happened when an aqueduct burst its banks to reveal a large head of gudgeon which no-one ever caught.

Most coarse species are found in the canal but roach, rudd, bream, tench, perch and carp are predominant. Carp are present in large numbers thanks to Warrington AA who control several miles. The association has injected thousands of common and mirrors to 5lb, many of which have grown into double-figures. In fact, most matches these days are won with one or two carp around the 7lb mark, though many bigger fish are lost on the light tackle necessary to attract bites.

A typical northern canal in the industrial heartland of the North. This stretch of the Leigh Canal at Astley Green produces plenty of fish despite the dour surroundings

Caster is by far the best bait for these Bridgewater carp but one or two individuals have had some success with sweet corn. The favourite area for these bonny fighters is probably at Grappenhall, with Astley and Agden also producing a fair number. Rudd are beginning to make their presence felt in various stretches and, again, these fish were introduced by Warrington AA. Perch, which were once prolific in many lengths and then disappeared, are coming back in the Leigh area. Most bream are taken from between Preston Brook and Runcorn, a stretch that also produces a few tench.

Licence – North West Water Authority.

Where to Fish:
Runcorn to Preston Brook. Halton Joint Anglers have this stretch and, though no day tickets are issued, season permits can be obtained from the secretary Mr W. Durr, Footbridge Cottage, Canal Street, Runcorn.

Preston Brook to Broadheath Bridge, Altrincham. Warrington AA control this lengthy piece and again, although there are no day tickets, membership is open to anyone through the secretary Mr Stan Jackson, 23 Nora Street, Warrington.

Broadheath Bridge to Leigh. One arm of the canal runs into Manchester as far as Corn Brook Bridge. This water is controlled by Northern AA who issue day tickets through patrolling bailiffs. The length between Manchester and Leigh is governed by Northern AA and Leigh and District AA and day tickets are available on the towpath or from local tackle dealers. Northern AA secretary is Mr G. Wilson, 11 Guildford Avenue, Chorley, and Leigh and District AA secretary, Mr J. Scotson, 28 Glover Street, Leigh, Lancs.

Calder and Hebble Navigation

Cut to link the Rochdale, Huddersfield and Leeds–Liverpool Canals, the Calder and Hebble Navigation runs from Sowerby Bridge via Wakefield to join the Aire and Calder Navigation at Castleford. A typical industrial canal, it is polluted by factory waste in parts but fish, mainly roach and gudgeon, are caught in many areas. As one club official put it: 'We are optimists, and occasionally our enthusiasm bears fruit in the shape of a 1lb roach, but usually we have little to show for our efforts.'

Licence – Yorkshire Water Authority.

Where to Fish:
There are no day ticket facilities on this canal, though some of the clubs and associations with holdings are open for membership.

Clubs and Secretaries:
Bradford No. 1 AA. Mr C. Smith, 44 Fleet Lane, Queensbury, Bradford.
Brighouse AA. Mr T.A. Riley, 16 Coronation Terrace, Greetland, Nr Halifax, W. Yorks.

Dean Clough AS. Mr C.R. Crabtree, 20 Overden Avenue, Halifax.

Macintosh AC. Mr R. Russell, 2 Barrington Close, South-owram, Halifax.

N.E. Gas Board AC. Mr J.A. Mitchell, Sports Club, Leeds Road, Huddersfield.

Slaithwaite & District AA. Mr A. Bamforth, 43 Binn Road, Marsden, Huddersfield.

Unity AC. Mr K.E. Mann, 19 Busfield Street, Bradford.

Chesterfield Canal

A narrow canal cut to link Chesterfield with the River Trent, the Chesterfield runs for about 20 miles from the town of its name to West Stockwith on the Trent. It is unnavigable and neglected between Chesterfield and Worksop but from there on fishing is excellent in many areas.

The canal became famous in 1978 and received national publicity when workmen accidentally pulled out a centuries-old plug draining a large section near Retford, Notts., leaving several boats stranded. Fortunately the fish survived and sport has not suffered to any great extent.

Noted for its specimen bream to 6lb, carp to 14lb and quality roach and tench which are caught regularly, the Chesterfield is unusual in that it also holds a fair head of chub. These run up to 5lb and are concentrated mainly in the Ranby area near Retford. Pleasure bags of up to 20lb have been taken and one of the best baits is wasp grub. Worksop & District AAA and Worksop United AA have re-stocked with roach and bream several times in the last few years and fish have also been injected by the Severn–Trent Authority.

Licence – Severn–Trent Water Authority.

Where to Fish:
Although some of the fishing is for club members only, many lengths are available on day tickets.
Shireoaks to Bracebridge Lock. Grafton AA issue day tickets on the towpath for this section.

Bracebridge to Ranby. Worksop United AA control the rights from High Hoe Road, Worksop to Humped Back Bridge, Ranby. No day tickets are available but limited seasonal permits are issued.

Ranby to Retford. Retford AA lease 5¼ miles from Chequers Bridge, Ranby to Woodcock Bridge, Retford. No day tickets are issued but membership is open to a limited number of residents on a first-come-first-served basis.

Retford to Clayworth. Worksop and District AAA have the rights from West Retford Bridge to Church Lane, Clayworth. Day tickets are available on the towpath.

Drakeholes to West Stockwith. Sheffield and District AA have this stretch, day tickets for which can be obtained from the lock keeper, Gringley, Notts.

Clubs and Secretaries:
Grafton AA. Mr R.A. Mee, 157 Ariston Avenue, Worksop, Notts.
Kiveton Park AA. Mr H. Edge, 7 Lambrell Green, Kiveton Park, Sheffield.
Renishaw Iron Co. Ltd AC. c/o Renishaw Iron Co. Ltd, Renishaw, Sheffield, S. Yorks.
Retford AA. Mr H. Oxby, 104 Moorgate, Retford, Notts.
Sheffield & District AA. Mr J.W. Taylor, Station Hotel, Wicker, Sheffield 3.
Worksop & District AAA. Mr G.D. Rollinson, 31 Lincoln Street, Worksop, Notts.
Worksop United AA. Mr R. Whitehead, 72 Dryden Dale, Worksop, Notts.

Forth and Clyde Canal

Constructed to connect the River Clyde with the North Sea, the Forth and Clyde Canal cuts straight across Scotland stretching from the Firth of Forth via Glasgow to meet the River Clyde at Bowling, near Dumbarton. The canal is no longer used for commercial boat traffic, indeed several sections have been filled in, become overgrown or silted up.

Because there are no close season restrictions on coarse fishing in Scotland, the Forth and Clyde has become a Mecca for English anglers between the months of March and June. Several big contests, including the Scottish National Championship, are held during this period and they attract large entries from South of the Border.

Fishing in recent years has become rather patchy in many sections, though plenty of good roach, smaller roach, small perch and hordes of 'jack' pike, are taken in matches. Tench and carp are also caught in some lengths.

Deep, up to eight feet in places, and very wide, the Forth and Clyde calls for river-style tactics with waggler floats or light leger tackle fished well across. Casters and bronze maggots are the most popular baits for match fishing but pleasure anglers take good bags on other offerings particularly breadflake and worms.

No rod licence is required.

Where to Fish:
Glasgow and West of Scotland CAA control seven miles between Banknock and Twechar with day ticket facilities. Edinburgh and East of Scotland CAA have 1½ miles from Castle Cary to Bonnybridge, for which day tickets are available. Kirkintilloch Angling Club lease 2½ miles (day tickets available) from Old Kilpatrick to Bowling. The remainder of the canal is controlled by the British Waterways Board. Season permits issued.

Huddersfield Narrow Canal

This canal, which runs from Yorkshire into Lancashire, links the Calder and Hebble Navigation with the Ashton and Peake Forest Canals at a point on the outskirts of Manchester. Almost twenty miles in length, the Huddersfield Narrow is famous for its tunnel at Standedge which is 5,698 yards long, and is the longest tunnel in the country.

Although sport can be very patchy, especially in contests,

this canal has produced some outstanding catches over the years. Parts of the Lancashire length, for instance, hold trout which suggests that the water quality is first class. The canal is actually very clear with a lot of weed in some sections which provides the ideal surroundings for the carp introduced by clubs. These fish are growing at a good rate and a number up to 9lb have been landed.

In recent years sweet corn has accounted for quite a few. Other species present are roach, bream, tench and perch. The latter species, so rare in many canals these days, thrive in the Huddersfield and it's not unusual to take seven or eight pounds of them at a sitting.

Licence – Yorkshire Water Authority from Huddersfield to Standedge Tunnel
North-West Water Authority from the other side of the tunnel to Manchester.

Where to Fish:
Huddersfield to Standedge Tunnel. Slaithwaite & District AS control seven miles from Longroyd Bridge to Tunnel End, Marsden. Day tickets can be had, in advance, from the secretary, The Angling Centre, Chapel Hill, Huddersfield, or from The Albion Inn, Longroyd Bridge.
Saddleworth & District AS take over at the Lancashire end of the tunnel with rights from Lock 30 to Lock 24. The club also have a stretch at Mossley from Bridge 85 to Lock 9. Day tickets are available for both sections.
Oldham & District control from Lock 24 (Saddleworth) to Bridge 85 at Greenfields. Day tickets are obtainable from local tackle shops or on the towpath.
Ashton-under-Lyne. Dukinfield Astley AC lease the length between Locks 1 and 9 which extends from Ashton-under-Lyne to Hartshead Power Station, Staleybridge. Day and season permits available.

Clubs and Secretaries:
Dukinfield Astley AS. Mr P. Hill, 174 Chapel Street, Dukinfield, Cheshire.

Oldham & District AAA. Mr H. Garside, 60 Queensway, Greenfield, Saddleworth, Oldham, Lancs.

Saddleworth & District AS. Mr C.T. Johnson, 3 Birch Road, Uppermill, Oldham, Lancs.

Slaithwaite & District AS. Mr A. Bamforth, 43 Binn Road, Marsden, Huddersfield.

Lancaster Canal

Stretching from Preston, Lancs., in the south to just below Kendal, in Cumbria, the Lancaster Canal is unusual in that it doesn't connect with any other canal system, although there is an arm at Galgate linking it with the River Lune estuary at Glasson.

Seventy miles in length, the canal is an important North-West match fishery but there is plenty of room for pleasure anglers. Most fishing takes place between Preston and Carnforth. Above Carnforth it has been neglected with many lengths becoming silted up and choked with weed.

Roach, bream, tench, perch and pike are the main species but, as in most of our Northern canals, the fish rarely attain much by way of size. The numerous basins or boat lay-bys along the canal offer the best chances of bags of bream to 4lb.

Light legering, well across, offering maggot or breadflake on a small hook, is the most popular method. Tench fishing has improved in recent years with some excellent summer catches being reported from stretches around Forton and Cabus. Chub seem to be established at Forton, and bream of up to 5lb have been taken from the basins. Perch can also be expected from most lengths, thanks to the Northern AA who injected 33,000 in batches of 1000 to every mile of canal in 1976. Stocking is now controlled by the University of Salford, Biological Department, which monitors fish stocks regularly in an effort to maintain a good balance.

Match tactics are generally dominated by bloodworm styles which account for tiny bream, ruffe and roach, with the occasional larger fish. Punched bread also scores on some lengths.

Licence – North West Water Authority.

Where to Fish:
Northern Anglers Association control the whole of the fishing, including the Glasson Arm. Day tickets are available in advance.

Clubs and Secretaries:
Northern AA. Mr G. Wilson, 11 Guildford Avenue, Chorley, Lancs.

Leeds and Liverpool Canal

An amazing achievement in canal engineering, the Leeds and Liverpool is almost 130 miles long and passes over the Pennine Hills on its cross-country route from Liverpool via Wigan, Chorley, Blackburn, Burnley and Skipton to Leeds.

Wide, and with a good depth around five feet, the Lancashire section is the pride of the north-west anglers. Dozens of major contests are held between Liverpool and Chorley and results have been so good in recent years that the canal has been put forward as a venue for the NFA Championship.

Roach, tench and bream are the main species, though the quantity, and subsequent sport, varies from section to section. Massive re-stocking by the Lancashire associations who control the fishing is paying dividends and, despite occasional losses through pollution, all in all the Leeds and Liverpool seems to be getting better every year. There are still a few black spots, however, such as between Blackburn and Burnley where the acidity of the water drained in from the Pennine Moors affects the fish.

In Yorkshire, the Leeds and Liverpool Canal AA are doing excellent work to improve the fishing. A lot of re-stocking has taken place over the past few years and more is planned in a bid to bring the Yorkshire sections on a par with those in Lancashire. One of the best stretches in Lancashire is between Liverpool and Halsall. Feature fish here are tench which grow fat in the heavily weeded gin-clear water to give great sport during the summer.

A typical scene on the Leeds–Liverpool Canal, as it runs through a built-up area. The towpath provides easy access, especially for local youngsters without transport

Unlike on other canals you don't have to fish fine. One of the most popular methods is a big lump of bread on a size 10 hook, laid hard on, close in. In winter, roach are caught on casters offered well across. Match tactics are generally based on the middle to far shelf technique with bronze maggots, casters or punched bread the most successful baits.

One of the most popular pleasure stretches is near Aintree racecourse. Notable spots on this section are the Corn Mill at Maghull, the Drum factory at Lydiate and Scarisbrick Basin. Below Halsall, fishing is affected by the River Douglas which tops up the level near Wigan. Over the years this age-long-polluted river has been the cause of many fish kills but it has now been cleaned up and sport should improve in areas such as Gathurst, Crooke and Martland Mill. The Leigh Branch of the canal should also benefit from a cleaner River Douglas.

Above Wigan Locks the Leeds and Liverpool is known as the Haigh Canal and this length is now showing the most consistency for many years with good catches of bream, roach and odd tench. Around Johnson's Hillock Lock, gudgeon are prolific. From Chorley to Blackburn experimental contests have proved that the fish are returning following heavy pollution. In the Yorkshire lengths the stock fish tend to be much smaller than those over the border, but re-stocking is taking care of the situation.

Licence – Yorkshire Water Authority Licence from Foulbridge Tunnel, Yorkshire end.
North West Water Authority from the other end of the tunnel to Liverpool.

Where to Fish:
Liverpool to Halsall. Liverpool and District AA control thirty miles from the city centre to Halsall, for which day tickets can be obtained on the towpath.
Halsall to Wigan. Wigan DAA take over on this section as far as Johnson's Hillock Lock, a distance of 24 miles. The canal above Wigan Locks to Johnson's Hillock is known locally as the Haigh Canal. Day tickets for the whole of this section are available. At Johnson's Hillock Lock the fishing passes into the hands of the Northern AA. Day tickets on the towpath.
Blackburn to Gargrave. The Marsden Star AC have an eight mile length between the Northern AA and the Leeds and Liverpool Canal AA water, which starts at Bank Newton Top Lock, Gargrave, right on to Leeds. The Leeds/Liverpool Canal AA, a consortium of Northern associations, control the remaining 38 miles. It is all day-ticket water.
The Arm which runs from Wigan to Leigh to link the Bridgewater Canal (sometimes called the Leigh Canal) is mostly controlled by Leigh & District AA who issue day tickets through patrolling bailiffs.
Rufford Arm. This branch, linking the Leeds Liverpool with the River Douglas, is controlled by Liverpool DAA. Daytickets at the waterside.

Clubs and Secretaries:

Ashton & District Centre Northern AA. Mr R. Brown, 10 Dale Road, Golborne, Lancs.

Leeds and Liverpool Canal Anglers' Association. Mr S. Watmough, 8 Moor View Court, Sandbeds, Keighley, W. Yorks.

Leigh & District Association of Anglers. Mr J. Scotson, 26 Glover Street, Leigh, Lancs.

Liverpool & District AA. Mr J. Johnson, 97 Liverpool Road North, Maghull, Lancs.

Northern AA. Mr G.W. Wilson, 11 Guildford Avenue, Chorley, Lancs.

Saltaire AA. Mr W.M. Troman, 7 Hall Royd, Shipley, W. Yorks.

Wigan & District Centre Northern AA. Mr T.A. Blackledge, 16 Florence Street, Wigan, Lancs.

Leven Canal

Only 3½ miles long, the Leven Canal connects the village of Leven, in Yorkshire, with the River Hull near Aike. Clear and very weedy in parts, with an average depth of 3½ feet, it holds a good head of coarse fish, especially tench, which run up to 5lb. As a matter of fact, sizeable bags of smaller tench, fish around three-pound mark, are quite common in summer from any number of points along the canal. Bream, which average 3 to 4lb, are caught from more localised spots, but skimmers are likely to turn up anywhere. Roach, perch and rudd are also present in fair numbers, as well as a few carp and pike.

Licence – Yorkshire Water Authority

Where to Fish:

The whole of both banks of the canal, apart from two small private sections, is controlled by Hull AA. Secretary is Mr K. Bone, 44 Barrington Avenue, Cottingham Road, Hull, Yorkshire.

Day tickets and season permits can be purchased from tackle shops in Hull and Beverley.

Macclesfield Canal

Cut as part of the link between the Yorkshire canal system and the Trent and Mersey, the Macclesfield runs from a junction with the Peak Forest Canal at Marple, Cheshire, via Bollington, Macclesfield and Congleton to join the Trent and Mersey at Hardings Wood Junction north of Kidsgrove, Staffs.

Anyone who fished fifteen to twenty years ago will remember the canal as a famous roach water which produced scores of 2lb-plus specimens, particularly to Bollington big-fish-specialist Albert Oldfield. Albert regularly made the headlines in *Angling Times* with his noteworthy catches, which were mostly taken on lobworms and breadflake.

Like many other inland waterways, the Macclesfield then fell into a decline but the last few years have seen a remarkable come-back. Re-stocking (Prince Albert AS injected 50,000 mixed species in 1978) and a natural increase in stock fish, has boosted sport in many sections and there are signs that class roach have returned in numbers.

Bream, too, are thriving in the wides and basins. This was confirmed in 1978 when Cheshire angler David Orson netted over 50lb of good roach, plus bream to 2½lb at Higher Poynton. As on other canals, carp are also present and an 11-pounder was taken in 1978. In the Congleton area gudgeon appear to have multiplied considerably and they prove useful to match anglers. All in all the future of the Macclesfield looks very bright.

Licence – North West Water Authority

Where to Fish:
Northern AA have obtained the rights from the junction with the Peak Forest Canal at Marple (Cheshire) to Buxton Road Bridge, Macclesfield, but there is, at the time of writing, a dispute over the lease with British Waterways Board. When this is settled, day tickets will be available on the towpath.

Near Congleton, several clubs control short sections. Stoke-on-Trent have the fishing between bridges 61 and 68 but it is for members only. Kidsgrove offer day-ticket facilities for one mile between Bridges 72 and 75 (applications to the secretary). From Bridge 75 to Bridge 77 belongs to Congleton AS (day-tickets available). Adderley Green WMC limit their stretch between Bridges 79 and 80 to members only. The next section, to Bridge 80A, can be fished on day-ticket obtainable from the secretary of the Robin Hood AC. At Scholar Green (Staffs) Crewe LMR AS control 3½ miles from Watery Lane Aqueduct to Hall Green Lock, for which day tickets can be obtained on the towpath.

Clubs and Secretaries:
Adderley Green WMC AC. Mr W. Lawson, 70 St Mary's Road, Sandford Hill, Stoke-on-Trent.
Congleton AS. Mr N.J. Bours, 8 Norfolk Road, Congleton, Cheshire.
Crewe LMR Sports Club. Mr A. Jones, 290 Crewe Road, Gresty, Crewe.
Kidsgrove & District AS. Mr C.E. Woodcock, 29 Mitchell Avenue, Talke, Stoke-on-Trent.
Macclesfield Waltonian AS. Mr S.W. Shackley, Canal Bungalow, Bosley, Nr Macclesfield, Cheshire.
North Staffs AA. Mr C. Moore, 38 Debenham Crescent, Stoke-on-Trent.
Prince Albert AS. Mr C. Sparkes, High Lodge, Upton, Macclesfield.
Robin Hood AC. Mr K. Wilson, 52 Beach Drive, Kidsgrove, Stoke-on-Trent.
Stoke-on-Trent AS. Mr S.F. Broadgate, 5 Kingsfield Oval, Basford, Stoke-on-Trent.

Manchester, Bolton and Bury Canal

This short canal runs from Bury towards Bolton and is unconnected with any other waterway. Most of the original canal has been filled in and only a few miles of waterway are left. Very weedy in summer, the canal holds some nice fish, thanks mainly to the efforts of the Bolton and Bury angling clubs. The secretary of Bolton & District AA tells me his associates have spent over £2,500 during the last few years in a bid to improve sport but says they are beset by problems, and adds 'We seem to be fighting a losing battle.'

Licence – North West Water Authority.

Where to Fish:
Bury & District AA have two miles between Hinds Bridge, Elton, and Withins Bridge, Radcliffe. Day tickets available. Bolton & District AA have two sections, one between Baileys Bridge and Withins Bridge, and the other between Hall Lane and the filled-in section at Nob Hill, Little Lever. Day tickets are available.

Clubs and Secretaries:
Bolton & District AA. Mr A. Riding, 34 Higher Swan Lane, Bolton, Greater Manchester.
Bury & District AA. Mr F. Booth, 142 Bury Road, Tottington, Nr Bury, Lancs.

Market Weighton Canal

Running from Market Weighton to the Humber at Broomfleet Lock, a distance of six miles, this canal was once a famous match fishing venue, until sport deteriorated in the late sixties. These days the water produces quality roach and bream, plus odd chub, perch and dace though many early season contests are won with flounders and eels.

According to one regular visitor the canal is not sufficiently stocked as, despite having good days with up to 50lb of roach and bream at a sitting, these are overshadowed by too many blank outings. One problem, he claims, is the lack of liaison between anglers and the Yorkshire Water Authority, particularly with respect to control over the canal's flow and level. Apparently the lock gates are opened without warning, allowing the water to run off at a very fast rate, which ruins sport.

Licence – Yorkshire Water Authority

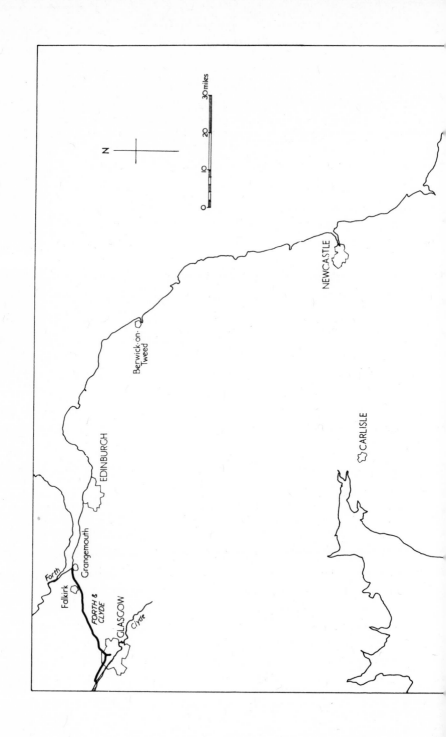

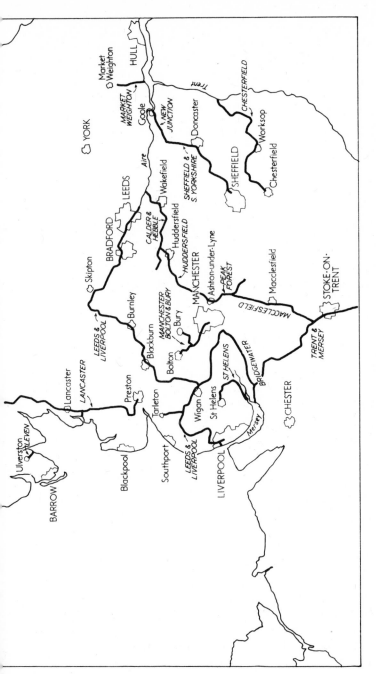

Canals of the North and Scotland

Where to Fish:
Fishing on both banks of the canal for the whole of its length is free to holders of a Yorkshire W.A. licence. Contests can be booked through the Authority at 37 North Bar Within, Beverley, Yorks.

New Junction

Providing a link between the Aire and Calder Navigation and the Sheffield and South Yorkshire Canal, the New Junction runs for 5½ miles from Cowick (Yorks) to Barnby Dun.

Polluted by ammonia, this canal is no longer the popular fishery it once was. Although good quality roach are caught occasionally they are few and far between. And apparently the ammonia content in the water inhibits their breeding, so until this is improved prospects appear poor.

Licence – Yorkshire Water Authority

Where to Fish:
Castleford & District AA control the whole of the canal. Day tickets can be obtained from the Lock Keeper at Sykehouse or any tackle dealer in the area who sells Castleford AA membership cards.

Secretary – Mr E. Ward, 54 Lynwood Crescent, Pontefract, W. Yorks.

Peak Forest Canal

Running from the Ashton Canal near Manchester, the Peak Forest passes through Marple, Cheshire, where it links up with the Macclesfield Canal and then continues to Whaley Bridge, a length of 14 miles.

As a fishery the Peak Forest can at best be described as very, very patchy, though the two controlling associations are making every effort to remedy the situation. Small roach, perch and gudgeon are the predominant species with carp and tench having been introduced in some sections. To learn

more of the canal's potential, Stockport Federation intend to
run a series of matches over their ten-mile length and then re-
stock those sections that are known to contain fish. Hyde &
District Federation are also carrying out an intensive programme.

Licence – North West W.A.

Where to Fish:
Hyde and District Federation have the rights from Ashton
Junction to Woodley Tunnel, a distance of four miles. Day
tickets can be obtained on the towpath. Stockport Federation
take over at the other end of the tunnel to Whaley Bridge.
Again, day tickets can be obtained at the waterside.

Clubs and Secretaries:
Hyde & District Federation of Anglers. Mrs B. Smart, 20
Kingston Gardens, Hyde, Cheshire.
Stockport & District Anglers' Federation. Mr C. Holland,
121 Northgate Road, Edgeley, Stockport, Cheshire.

St Helens Canal

Also known as the Sankey–St Helens Canal, this waterway
has a certain historical interest in that it was the very first
canal to be opened in England. Running from St Helens to
Sankey Brook on the River Mersey, it has, unfortunately,
fallen into a state of neglect, many sections having been filled
in. There are two main lengths which hold fish, one at
Newton le Willows and the other near St Helens. The Newton
le Willows piece has a see-saw history of pollution and the last
major calamity occurred in June, 1977, when trade effluent
wiped out thousands of fish in 1,200 yards of canal. It was a
tragic blow to Newton le Willows AA who control the rights
because the water had only just recovered from a similar
occurrence three years previously.

Following the latest pollution, the length was drained off,
refilled with clean water and re-stocked with roach, bream

and carp. These fish, along with those that escaped the pollution, are now thriving once again and providing good sport.
The St Helens length is also subject to pollution occasionally,
but around 2½ miles or so is in good condition and fishes
quite well. Part of this water is famous for catches of tropical
fish which seem to flourish in the warm water discharged by
factories in the area. Guppies, cichlids and other tropical varieties were introduced over twenty years ago by the proprietor
of an aquarist shop when he closed down and they now breed
and grow to a good size, providing sport throughout the
season. Elsewhere roach, bream, perch and carp are caught in
reasonable numbers.

Licence – North West W.A.

Where to Fish:
Newton le Willows AA control three quarters of a mile which
can be fished on a seasonal permit and day ticket obtainable
at the waterside.
St Helens AA have several miles in the area of the town. No
day tickets are issued but association membership is open to
anyone through the secretary Mr J. Powell, 49 Eskdale
Avenue, Car Mill, St Helens, Merseyside.

Sheffield and South Yorkshire Canal

Linking Sheffield and the River Don with the River Trent at
Keadby, the Sheffield and South Yorkshire Canal is a wide,
deep navigation (seventy feet wide and six feet deep in places)
that runs from Sheffield through Rotherham, Swinton, Conis-
borough, Mexborough, Doncaster, Thorne, and Crowle, to
its junction with the Trent at Keadby.

Badly polluted by the River Don some years ago, it is now
recovering and showing signs of the good fishing that once
attracted thousands of anglers, particularly to the sections
north of Doncaster. Catches of up to 30lb of roach and bream
have been reported quite recently from the Keadby area, but,
as one club official commented 'The canal is still very patchy

Steam rises from the water as these anglers fish the St Helens Canal in the heart of St Helens, Lancashire. Canal water is taken in by the Pilkington sheet glass factory to cool the rollers. The water, near boiling point, is then sprayed back into the canal, keeping the average water temperature along this stretch at nearly 70°F

and it could be a while before it regains its former reputation.' Nevertheless, small carp stocked five years ago have put on plenty of weight and when captured tip the scales at over 5lb, a real sign that the water quality is good. Winter match weights, in excess of 9lb, have also been reported.

The southern, or Sheffield end of the canal has always been subject to pollution from effluent discharged from the many factories and steelworks lining the towpath but the problem is now being contained and tests by the Yorkshire Water Authority have revealed the water to be in excellent condition and quite capable of supporting fish. Encouraged by this news, a number of Sheffield clubs have taken leases and re-stocked several miles of the Tinsley section. The first batch of 1,000 crucian carp and 2,000 roach was introduced in 1976 above and below the lock near The Plumpers Hotel at Tinsley.

Other consignments have since been injected in other

areas. The canal, and towpaths, have also been cleared of rubbish under a job creation scheme. Fishing in this area is still rather chancy, however, with a few roach, rudd, eels and small bream making up the bags, but a Tinsley club official has evidence of one or two double-figure catches of roach, which is very encouraging.

Licence – Severn–Trent W.A. from Crowle to Keadby. Yorkshire W.A. from Crowle to Sheffield.

Where to Fish:
The Stainforth and Keadby Joint Angling Committee, composed of Doncaster & District AA, Sheffield Amalgamated AS, Rotherham and District UAF, Scunthorpe and District AA, and British Rail Staff Association AS, lease 13¼ miles from Stainforth High Lock to Keadby Lock. Day tickets are available through the secretary Mr T. J. Dickens, 18 Burns Road, Herringthorpe, Rotherham. Other clubs with holdings are:– Woodseats WMC AC, secretary Mr W. D. Haley, 96 Abbey View Road, Sheffield, who have the rights between Bernard Road Bridge and Cadman Street Bridge. Between Locks 4 & 5 at Tinsley is leased by Firth Derihon Canal Angling & Social Club.
From Aqueduct, Worksop Road, to Coleridge Bridge is controlled by Fox House Canal Fishing Club, secretary Mr Alan Edwards, 78 Barber Road, Sheffield.
Keadby Power Station Social and Recreation Club control a short stretch, secretary Mr V. Watson, 16 Asquith Avenue, Ealand, Scunthorpe.
Shireoaks to Norwood. Kiveton Park AC. Secretary Mr H. Edge, 7 Lambrell Green, Kiveton Park, Nr Sheffield.
Shirland Lane to Stainforth Road. Sheffield Foundry Workers Club & Institute, 106 Beaumont Road North, Sheffield. Secretary Mr T. Berresford.
Stainforth Road Bridge to Bacon Lane Bridge. Spartan Sheffield Social Club AC. Secretary is Mr M. Dawson, 200 Newman Road, Wincobank, Sheffield.

Other small lengths: Swift Levick & Sons AC. Secretary Mr R. Drake, 443 Staniforth Road, Darnall, Sheffield; and Tuffnells AA, secretary is Mr B. Gunson, 121 Northern Avenue, Sheffield.

THE MAJOR CANALS: MIDLANDS

Ashby Canal

Also known as the Moira Canal, the Ashby runs from the Coventry Canal at Marston Junction, near Nuneaton, via Hinckley, Market Bosworth and Shackerstone to terminate at Snarestone, near Ashby, a distance of 26 miles. Clear and extremely weedy in parts, it holds plenty of small roach, gudgeon, bream and perch, plus tench in certain areas. Scene of many matches, the Ashby rarely produces spectacular weights but early morning and evening pleasure anglers take fair bags in the summer.

Licence – Severn–Trent W.A.

Where to Fish:
Bulkington. Coventry DAA lease the fishing from Bridges 1 to 11. Day tickets can be obtained on the towpath from patrolling bailiffs, or from local tackle dealers.
Hinckley. Hinckley DAA take over at Bridge 11 (Burton Hastings) to Bridge 20 (Wyken). No day tickets are issued but association membership is open to all. Coventry DAA have more fishing from Bridge 22 at Dadlington to Bridge 45 beyond Market Bosworth, except for a short piece between Bridges 44 and 45. Day tickets are available on the towpath.
Market Bosworth. Shackerstone AA take control at Bridge 58. Day tickets on the towpath or from the secretary.
Snarestone. Measham AC have two miles from the water works to Bridge 58. No day tickets but season permits are available.

Clubs and Secretaries:
Coventry DAA. Mr M. Williams, 134 Scots Lane, Coundon, Coventry.
Hinckley DAA. Mr L. Aston, 75 Forest Road, Hinckley, Leics.

Leicester & Dist. AA. R. Green, 52 Skampton Road, Leicester.
Measham Fishing Club. Mr J. Wainwright, 6 The Square,
Oakthorpe, Burton-on-Trent.
Shackerstone DAA. Mrs B. Andrews, 6 Church Road, Shack-
erstone, Nuneaton.

Beeston (Nottingham) Canal

This canal runs from Beeston Lock on the River Trent to
Lenton where it joins the Nottingham Canal. A really excellent fishery (13 species were discovered in a recent survey) it
is described by top Nottingham match angler Frank Barlow
as probably the best canal he has ever fished. According to
Frank you can fish anywhere with any style and practically
all baits, though casters and maggots are the most popular.

Roach, gudgeon and small bream form the bulk of catches
but bitterling, a species resembling tiny roach, are common,
as well as carp to 7lb. Small barbel too, are taken at the
Beeston end. With a good depth, around 5 feet, the canal
shelves only on the far side so rod-end tactics often score. And
because there is a steady flow, a lightly shotted stick float
works well. The best stretches are between Beeston and
Boots' factory although many fish are caught even in the
centre of Nottingham, at London Road.

Licence – Severn–Trent W.A.

Where to Fish:
The rights are controlled by Nottingham Federation and Nottingham AA who issue day tickets in advance through local
tackle dealers.

Clubs and Secretaries:
Nottingham Federation AS. Mr W. Belshaw, 17 Spring Green,
Clifton Estate, Nottingham.
Nottingham AA. Mr L. E. Simpson, 92 Main St, Bulwell, Not-
tingham.

An angler hooks into a good eel during a session on this tree-lined stretch of the Birmingham–Worcester Canal near Alvechurch, Worcestershire

Birmingham Canal Navigations

There are reputed to be 112 miles of canals in and around Birmingham and the system is generally described as the Birmingham Canal Navigations or BCN for short. The network winds in and out of the Birmingham area linking towns in the Black Country and more urban parts of the West Midlands with the main canals which converge on the Second City.

While several of the canals are badly polluted by factory effluent and support no fish life whatsoever, others are of surprisingly good quality and hold plenty of fish, including some of specimen size. The British Waterways Board can take much of the credit for this as they stocked several lengths with carp, bream and roach a few years ago. These fish, especially the carp (mirrors and common) seem to be thriving, according to reports, although it is difficult to draw a clear picture as, despite the number of anglers in the West Midlands many of the canals are rarely fished.

BCN – Birmingham Canal

Running from near the centre of the city through industrial Smethwick and West Bromwich, the Birmingham Canal joins the Staffs–Worcester at Aldersley Junction, Wolverhampton.

While much of the waterway is polluted and has a horrible colour (it is deep green at Tipton and Great Bridge) the water quality improves considerably at the Wolverhampton end and a few fish are found in pockets.

Licence – Severn–Trent W.A.

Where to Fish:
None of this canal is leased to clubs and, in effect, the fishing is controlled by British Waterways Board. But, as there is no reference to the waterway in the Board's lists, it can presumably be regarded as free fishing. Certainly few anglers would wish to pay to fish this canal in its present condition.

BCN – Rushall Canal and Daw End Branch

This narrow waterway runs from the Tame Valley Canal at Rushall Junction, near Walsall, to join the Wyrley–Essington Canal near Brownhills. Once a noted roach water, this canal has never recovered from the fish diseases of the '60s. Also it has been subject to some surface pollution by oil in recent years. Nevertheless the water is crystal clear in parts especially south of Rushall and fish are coming back gradually.

British Waterways Board introduced thousands of carp, bream and roach in 1972, and these have spread to provide reasonable sport for anglers willing to explore different lengths. Many double-figure carp are hooked in the summer months. The best authenticated of these is a fish of 12lb which was landed near The Lock House, Park Hall, Walsall. From Daw End to Brownhills, fishing is very patchy and several experimental contests have been won with ounces.

Licence – Severn–Trent W.A.

Where to Fish:
British Waterways Board control many miles, day or season
tickets for which can be obtained from patrolling bailiffs.
Contests can be booked through the British Waterways Board
Bailiff, Lock House Cottage, Park Hall Road, Walsall, or Mr
J. Desmond, 93 Longwood Cottages, Rushall Top Lock,
Aldridge Road, Walsall.

The remainder is leased to clubs who do not issue day
tickets but allow occasional competitions.

Clubs and Secretaries:
Stinchcombe and Cooper AC. Mr P. Markham, Northgate,
Aldridge, Walsall, West Midlands.
Wednesfield AA. Mr J. E. Davies, 62 Windsor Gardens, Cast-
lecroft, Wolverhampton.

BCN – Tame Valley Canal

This canal runs from the Birmingham–Fazeley Junction at
Salford, Birmingham, to meet the Walsall Canal at Doe Bank
Junction, near West Bromwich. Like the Rushall Canal, the
Tame Valley is no longer the fishery it once was, but fish can
be found in patches particularly between Rushall Junction
and Great Barr. Small roach are the predominant species
though better-class fish, including carp (introduced by British
Waterways Board) turn up occasionally.

Licence – Severn–Trent W.A.

Where to Fish:
Most of the canal is controlled by British Waterways Board
with tickets available from bailiffs. Club fishing is reserved for
members only.

Clubs and Secretaries:
Barn Social Club AC. Mr H. Hulme, Brookvale Road, Witton,
Birmingham 6.
St Martins Kingfisher AC. Mr F. Pear, 27 Hastings Road,
Perry Common, Birmingham.

BCN – Walsall Canal

This waterway links the Birmingham Canal with the Wyrley and Essington and runs from Padding Green Junction, near West Bromwich, to Birchills Junction, Walsall. Subject to pollution from factory discharges, the Walsall Canal nevertheless holds fish especially at the Walsall end. Quality roach, plus small ones, with odd perch and bream, are the main species. The most popular area is near Walsall Power Station.

Licence – Severn–Trent W.A.

Where to Fish:
British Waterways Board have the rights, apart from lengths leased to two clubs. These reserve fishing for members only.

Clubs and Secretaries:
James Bridge Steelworks AS. The Angling Secretary, F.H. Lloyd & Co Limited Canteen, The Steelworks, Park Lane, Wednesbury, West Midlands.
H. R. Turner AC. Mr P. Washbrook, 2 Hawthorne Road, Short Heath, Willenhall, West Midlands.

BCN – Wyrley and Essington Canal

This navigation joins the Birmingham Canal at Horseley Fields Junction, near Wolverhampton, with the Daw End Branch of the Rushall Canal at Brownhills.

Gin-clear for most of its length, this canal is the best of the BCN network and holds quite a good head of fish in certain stretches. The Cannock and Anglesey extensions, which run from Pelsall and Brownhills, also support several species. Because of the clarity of the water the fish are difficult to catch, however, as match anglers will confirm. But results from pleasure or individual anglers who fish late in the evening or in the early morning tell a different story and there are many tales of bags of quality roach, plus big carp and tench, and occasional bream.

The Cannock extension is reputed to have produced a 17lb carp, but this section is perhaps much better known for its large head of 'jack' pike and tench. Popular spots are between New Invention and Brownhills but the area around Pelsall Wood is probably the most prolific.

Against a bleak winter landscape, anglers fish a small club match on the Wyrley–Essington Canal at Pelsall, West Midlands

Licence – Severn–Trent W.A.

Where to Fish:
The whole of the canal, plus the two extensions, is leased to clubs, most of which allow day ticket or contest facilities. Cannock Extension, Pelsall. Edward Street WMC AC control most of this length, day tickets or season permits available from the secretary, or Mr Coyne, Pelsall Stop, Canal Side, Pelsall.

Brownhills. L.C.P. Steel Products AC have three quarters of a mile from High Bridge to Becks Bridge approximately 100 pegs). Tickets from bailiff on towpath, season cards and contest bookings through the secretary.

Pelsall. Albion Pressed Metal AC have the fishing from Pelsall Junction to Pelsall Works Bridge. Day tickets from the secretary. From Pelsall Works Bridge to Fishley Turnover Bridge is controlled by the Freemasons AC. Day tickets from secretary.

New Invention. Swan AC control a lengthy stretch from Lane Head towards Wednesfield. Day tickets from the secretary.

Wednesfield. Whitmore Reans AA lease the rights between Ward's Bridge and Heath Town. Day tickets from secretary.

Ward's Bridge to Perry Hall Bridge is controlled by Jenks & Cattell AC. Day tickets from secretary.

Clubs and Secretaries:
Albion Pressed Metal AC. Mr P. Weaver, 21 Harrison Road, Cannock, Staffs.
Edward St. WMC AC. Mr I.H. Jones, 101 Edward Street, Broomhill, Cannock, Staffs.
Freemasons AC. Mr J.D. Fletcher, 22 Benton's Lane, Great Wyrley, Walsall, West Midlands.
GKN–Sankey WMC AC. Mr A.R.Hopkins, 147 Ogley Road, Brownhills, Walsall, West Midlands.
James Bridge Copper Social Club AC. Mr J.H. Bird, c/o IMI Refiners Limited, James Bridge Copper Works, Darlaston Road, Walsall.

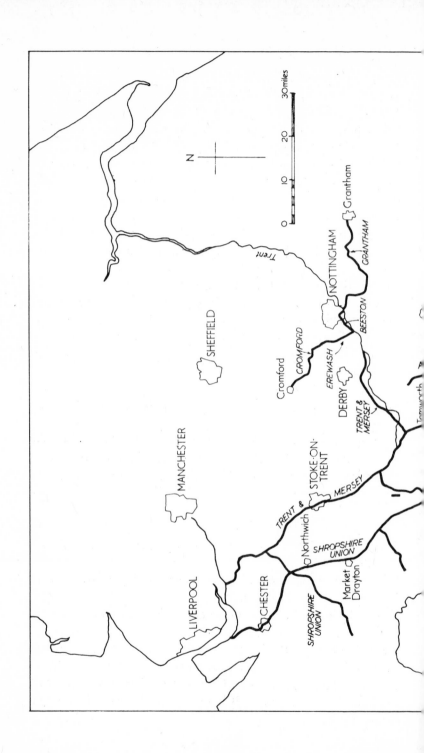

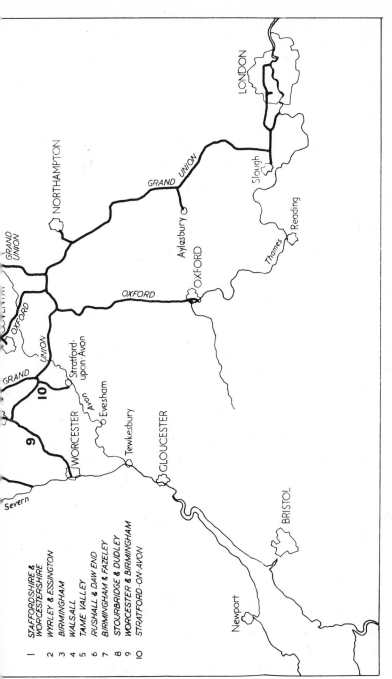

Canals of the Midlands

1   STAFFORDSHIRE &
      WORCESTERSHIRE
2   WYRLEY & ESSINGTON
3   BIRMINGHAM
4   WALSALL
5   TAME VALLEY
6   RUSHALL & DAW END
7   BIRMINGHAM & FAZELEY
8   STOURBRIDGE & DUDLEY
9   WORCESTER & BIRMINGHAM
10   STRATFORD-ON-AVON

Jenks & Cattell AC. Mr T.C. Gilson, 25 Reedley Road, Sneyd Park, Essington, Wolverhampton.

L.C.P. Steel Products AC. Mr W.H. Day, 56 Willenhall Street, Darlaston, West Midlands.

Newey (Tipton) AC. Mr E.A. Icke, 35 Waterfield Close, Tipton, West Midlands.

New Invention Victory Club AC. Mr C. Gaunt, 1 Brereton Road, New Invention, Willenhall, West Midlands.

Norton Canes Docks AC. Mr J. Yates, Yates Bros Limited, Lime Lane, Pelsall, Walsall, West Midlands.

Saddlers Arms AC. Mr B. Knight, 95 Bentley Lane, Old Birchills, Walsall, West Midlands.

Swan AC. Mr J. Wakelin, 68 High Road, Lane Head, Willenhall, West Midlands.

Whitmore Reans CAA. Mr R.H. Hughes, Star Chambers, Princes Square, Wolverhampton, West Midlands.

Birmingham and Fazeley Canal

This canal links the Trent and Mersey and Coventry Canals with the Grand Union. Starting at Gravelly Hill, near 'Spaghetti Junction', it runs through Tyburn and out of the city past Curdworth and on to Fazeley, near Tamworth, where it joins the Coventry Canal at Fazeley Junction. From here it flows through Hopwas and Whittington, near Lichfield, to terminate at Huddlesford Junction.

Rod Licence – Severn–Trent W.A.

A late recoverer from the fish disease of the 1960s, the Birmingham–Fazeley has only recently begun to show signs of its former glory, when big catches of roach, bream and perch were commonplace. Neglected and a bit of an eyesore at the Birmingham end where it is lined with factories and warehouses, it nevertheless produces fish, mainly roach, even in the shadow of 'Spaghetti Junction'. Elsewhere small roach, skimmer bream, and gudgeon are returning in fair numbers especially around Fazeley, Hopwas and Whittington.

Proof of the canal's improvement came in 1978 when it was used in the Birmingham AA Annual contest for the first time in years. Pegged at the Fazeley end, all the 200 entries or so caught fish and many weighed in more than 1lb.

Where to Fish:
Birmingham AA control all the fishing apart from a 1-mile length at Fazeley which belongs to Fazeley Victory Working Men's Club Angling Society. The BAA rights are for members only but tickets for the Fazeley Victory water can be obtained on the towpath.

Birmingham and Worcester Canal

This canal links Birmingham with the River Severn at Worcester and is also connected to the Stratford-on-Avon Canal at Kings Norton Junction. Starting in almost the centre of Birmingham, the canal leaves the suburbs at Kings Norton and cuts south to Alvechurch. Skirting Bromsgrove and Droitwich it passes through many picturesque villages in its way to join the Severn in the centre of Worcester.

A Mecca for Birmingham anglers, the Birmingham–Worcester was once one of the most prolific canals in the Midlands. Before fish disease struck in the mid sixties it simply teemed with roach, perch, gudgeon and bream, plus big carp, tench and pike, and you could be certain of excellent sport along practically any length.

The decline came suddenly around 1967 and then followed several years of ever-diminishing catches before returns began to improve. Unfortunately, this improvement has not been consistent and several lengths have come back into form only to deteriorate once again a couple of years later. A bright note is the fact that fish appear to be thriving in parts of the Birmingham end of the canal. There have been many reports of good catches in the Kings Norton area. The most popular sections, however, are south of Bromsgrove, from Dunhampstead Tunnel to Blackpole, above Worcester. Small roach and bream are the predominant species in this length, though

An angler fishes a stretch of Scotland's Forth and Clyde Canal

larger fish turn up frequently. In fact, bream to 5lb are not unusual in some lengths, notably Hanbury Wharfe, Oddingley, Tibberton and Stoke Works.

Breadflake, laid hard on the bottom, is the best method for attracting these specimens. Carp have always been a feature of the Birmingham–Worcester and many double figure fish have been landed over the years, especially from the Bromsgrove area. Smaller carp, up to 5lb, introduced by the Birmingham AA and Severn–Trent W.A. at various times, are now present in many lengths. These are frequently hooked and lost by match anglers, though if one is landed it is usually enough to win a contest.

Rod licence – Severn–Trent W.A.

Where to Fish:
Birmingham AA and Worcester DUAA control practically the whole of the fishing rights. The BAA's holdings start at the southern mouth of Kings Norton Tunnel and extend for 25 miles to Bridge 19 at Blackpole near Worcester. Worcester DUAA water starts at the BAA boundary and continues to the junction with the River Severn. Neither associations issue day tickets but membership is open to anyone.

Coventry Canal

Cut to link Coventry with the Trent and Mersey via the Birmingham–Fazeley, the Coventry Canal forms a vital link in the Midland system connecting also the Ashby Canal at Marston Junction and the Oxford at Hawkesbury.

Once a famous match fishery that produced excellent catches of roach, perch, bream and gudgeon, it suffered in the mid sixties the same fate as other Midland canals and has never fully recovered. Some sections around the Tamworth and Polesworth area have improved tremendously in recent years, though other lengths, particularly towards Coventry, can only be said to be very patchy.

Licence – Severn–Trent W.A.

Where to Fish:
Coventry & District AA have 21 miles from the junction at Hawkesbury to the Bulls Head Bridge at Polesworth. Day tickets can be purchased on the towpath from patrolling bailiffs. Tamworth WMC take over at the Coventry DAA boundary for six miles as far as Fazeley Bridge. Day and season permits for this section can be obtained from the secretary. Around Streethay several clubs lease short lengths and most offer day ticket facilities.

Clubs and Secretaries:
Coventry & District AA. Mr M. Williams, 134 Scots Lane, Coundon, Coventry.
Joseph Lucas AC. Mr D. Jackson, 19 Hayes View Drive, Cheslyn Hay, Walsall, West Midlands.
Tamworth WMC. Mr R. Whitehouse, Woodlands Close, Dordon, Near Tamworth, Staffs.
Vine Inn AC. Mr J.R. Booth, 1 Burnthill Lane, Rugeley, Staffs.
Whittington Social Club FC. Mr S.M. Arkless, 80 Spring Lane, Whittington, Near Lichfield, Staffs.

Canals can provide top quality fishing in beautiful surroundings, as this stretch of the Birmingham–Worcester Canal at King's Norton, Birmingham, testifies

Cromford Canal

Eighteen miles in length, the Cromford Canal runs from a junction with the Erewash Canal (Notts) to Cromford in Derbyshire. Neglected and derelict in most areas, it is now being restored by Derby County Council.

As a fishery it can only be described as very poor with fish few and far between, but Derby Railway Institute FC, who lease a lengthy stretch, intend to re-stock when the restoration is completed.

Licence – Severn–Trent W.A.

Where to Fish:
Derby Railway Institute Fishing Club hold a lease on several Derbyshire sections but more as a long term investment than for any present benefits.

Clubs and Secretaries:
Mr K. Ottewell, 65 Leytonstone Drive, Mackworth, Derby.

Erewash Canal

This canal is 12 miles long and runs from Langley Mill in Derbyshire to link up with the River Trent at Trent Lock near Long Eaton.

Although badly polluted a few years back the stock fish survived, and fair to excellent sport can now be had in many parts. Some re-stocking has also helped. Sizeable bream, tench around the 1lb mark plus occasional three-pounders, lots of roach and gudgeon, and carp into double-figures, make up catches though, according to well-known Long Eaton expert Aubrey Wainwright, who lives within a stone's throw of the water, the Erewash isn't fished a great deal.

Gin-clear throughout the summer, the canal is affected by the River Trent and colours up in the winter, particularly when the Trent is in flood. But this doesn't spoil the fishing. It is possible to catch two or three pounds of small stuff even when the water is the colour of chocolate. In summer the fish are not easy to tempt because of the clear water, but evening two-hour sweepstakes around the Ilkeston area frequently produce bags of five or six pounds.

Most carp are taken at Sandiacre and towards Stanton, and though a fair number up to 12lb have been landed, much bigger ones have escaped. These monsters can often be spotted rolling or basking on the surface on summer evenings. In recent years many chub to 2lb and hefty dace have been caught from spots where brooks or pipes running in to the canal create an extra flow.

Licence – Severn–Trent W.A.

Where to Fish:
Practically the whole of the canal can be fished on day-ticket or season permit. In the Long Eaton area tickets for the Long Eaton Federation AA and Long Eaton Victoria AS lengths can be obtained from local tackleists. At Trowell the Horse and Groom AC allow permit fishing on their 3½-mile stretch between Barkers and Whitehouse Locks. Above Whitehouse Lock, at Sandiacre, the Sandiacre Alexandra FC offer day ticket facilities as far as Sandiacre Lock. Near Langley Mill tickets can be obtained for the NCB No. 5 Area FC waters which run to Shipley Lock. Below this lock the Cotmanhey AC water extends to Barkers Lock, where tickets can be had from patrolling bailiffs.

Clubs and Secretaries:
Cotmanhey AC. Mr E. Stratham, 169 Ladywood Road, Ilkeston, Derbyshire.
Horse and Groom AC. Mr A.A. Bishop, 13 Hazel Drive, Larkhill Estate, Nuthall, Notts.
Long Eaton & Dist. Federation of Anglers. Mr W. Parker, 75 College Street, Long Eaton, Notts.
Long Eaton Victoria AS. Mr G. Plummer, 18 Sandford Avenue, Long Eaton, Notts.
NCB No. 5 Area Fishing Club. Mr D.A. Allsop, 27 Hardy Barn, Shipley, Derbyshire.
Sandiacre Alexandra Fishing Club. Mr E. Jones, Sudbury Avenue, Sandiacre, Derbyshire.

The Grand Union Canal

The longest canal constructed in England, the Grand Union is 94 miles in length and runs from the River Thames in London to Birmingham. It also connects, via a major arm, with Leicester where it joins the River Soar. Other arms or branches are at Paddington, Wendover, Aylesbury, Buckingham and Northampton. The Grand Union also connects with the Oxford and Stratford-on-Avon Canals.

Fishing on this canal varies from excellent to very poor,

depending on the area, but generally sport is as good if not better than most other narrow waterways.

Running southwards from Birmingham the Grand Union is of poor fishing quality until it reaches Catherine De Barnes in Warwickshire. Here sport improves with gudgeon and quality roach predominating. At Rowington, skimmer bream, roach, gudgeon and carp are plentiful with double-figure bags on the cards. The same species are found through Hatton, near Warwick, and on to Leamington, a stretch that has produced 20lb bags of tench, perch, bream and roach in recent years. Sport in this area is first class.

Napton to Norton Junction is rather patchy but good bags of the usual species are taken by pleasure anglers. From Norton Junction to Newport Pagnell first-class sport can be had with bream, tench and roach. Indeed, pleasure anglers think nothing of catching 20lb of bream in certain parts of this length. Specimen roach over 2lb are also taken, usually on cheese, while big eels, 4lb plus, are not uncommon.

Britain's longest canal, the Grand Union, at Watford

Below the canal junction with the River Tove, chub also appear from time to time. Newport Pagnell to Marsworth is a popular section with match anglers, who catch bream, roach and carp often running into double figures. South towards Marsworth the canal fishes well throughout the season with roach, bream, gudgeon, perch, rudd and carp. The latter species has exploded in recent years and, besides hordes of small samples, really big fish are hooked such as a 17lb 2oz fish landed in 1975.

Bream are more common north of Leighton Buzzard and match weights in excess of 25lb have been taken. From Marsworth to Tring the Grand Union has produced some notable catches including bream to 7lb and huge bags of small carp. Big roach and tench can also be expected.

Below Tring and on to Kings Langley, roach are the dominant species but tench, bream and carp add excitement to an outing. Carp can be caught in winter in the warm water discharged by the Ovaltine factory at Kings Langley.

South of Kings Langley and on to Rickmansworth chub occasionally figure among the more usual catches of roach, gudgeon and carp. From Rickmansworth to Denham deeper water contains plenty of roach up to the 1lb mark, bream and carp running into double figures. Dace and chub from the River Colne, which enters the canal in this area, also give good sport.

South of Denham and on to West Drayton, the Grand Union has a considerable flow due to the influence of the River Colne. This is good winter fishing. Below West Drayton the canal passes through built-up industrial areas as it runs into London. But, despite the grim surroundings, anglers catch quality roach, bream, gudgeon, carp and tench.

Licences: The Grand Union passes through several different Water Authority areas so check before fishing.

Where to fish:
Knowle. Coleshill DAS from Bridge 78 to Bridge 71. Tickets on towpath.

Rowington. Massey Ferguson AC. Tickets on towpath.

Hatton. Birmingham AA (members only).

Warwick to Napton Lock. Royal Leamington Spa AA control 12 miles. Tickets on towpath.

Napton to Norton Junction. Coventry DAA water from junction with Oxford Canal to the Leicester Arm at Buckby. Day tickets available.

Norton Junction to Newport Pagnell. Coventry DAA water to Muscott Mill. Northampton Nene AC take over from Bridge 22 at Weedon to Bridge 62 at Yardley Gobion. Tickets from local tackle shops or on the towpath. The Britannia AC have the next section to Bridge 64. No day tickets but contests allowed.

Newport Pagnell to Marsworth. More Coventry DAA water starts at Bridge 92 at Fenny Stratford and continues to Bridge 100 at Stoke Hammond. Luton AA take over at Bridge 102 for several miles as far as Bridge 126 near Marsworth. Tickets available on towpath.

Marsworth to Tring. Tring Anglers – day tickets on towpath.

Tring to Kings Langley. London AA water – tickets from bailiff.

Kings Langley to Rickmansworth. Watford Piscators (members only) as far as Croxley where tickets are available on towpath.

Rickmansworth to Denham. Blenheim AS – tickets from bailiff.

Denham to West Drayton. London AA water – tickets available.

West Drayton to Paddington. Also London AA water available on day ticket.

Grand Union Leicester Branch. Norton Junction to Market Harborough. Coventry DAA, Rugby AA and Leicester Amalgamated share this length. Tickets are available on the towpath.

Market Harborough to Leicester. Leicester AS, Wigston AS, Leicester AC, Leicester DAS, control most of this section and much of the canal is available on day ticket.

Market Harborough Arm. Market Harborough AS have 6½

miles of this short arm and have heavily re-stocked it with different species. Tickets obtainable on towpath.

Slough Arm. London AA – tickets on towpath.

Aylesbury Arm. From Marsworth to Red House. Tring Anglers – tickets on towpath.

Red House to Aylesbury. A.C. Delco AS and Aylesbury Federation – tickets available.

Wendover Arm. Tring Anglers – tickets on towpath.

Bletchley and Fenny Stratford WMC lease the stretch between Bridges 81 and 92. Day or season tickets through the secretary.

Northampton Arm. From Bridge 3 to Bridge 6 (approximately 3 miles) – Northampton Castle AC. Day tickets in advance or on the towpath.

Clubs, Secretaries and Riparian Owners:
Grand Union (Main Line)

Mr K.C. Bailey, The Lock House, Cosgrove, Wolverton, Bucks.

Blenheim AS. Mr F.W. Lancaster, 20 Hilary Road, London W12.

Bletchley & Fenny Stratford WMC. Mr F. Evans, 1 Chandos Place, Bletchley, Milton Keynes.

Britannia AC. Mr C.W. Gray, 3 Coverack Close, Delapre, Northampton.

Central Association of London and Provincial Anglers Clubs. Mr J.C. Watts, 9 Kemble Road, Croydon, Surrey.

Mr W. Jeffrey, 24 Colindale Road, Northampton.

Galleon AC. Mr G.C. Young, 48 Rickley Lane, Milton Keynes.

Kings Langley AS. Mr A.D. Foulger, 10 Abbots Rise, Kings Langley, Herts.

London AA. Mr H.J. Wilson, 183 Hoe Street, Walthamstow, London E17.

Luton AC. Mr D.W. Rayner, 35 Stratton Gardens, Luton, Beds.

Milton Keynes AA. Mr M. Sando, 6 Kipling Drive, Newport Pagnell, Bucks.

North Bucks Division of Working Men's Clubs. Mr B. Carvell, 22 Windsor Street, Wolverton, Milton Keynes.

Northampton Nene AC. Mr S.H. Battison, 36 Church Way, Weston Favell, Northampton.

Raven AC. Mr E.G. Mears, 16 Broomhouse Road, Fulham, London.

Sceptre AC. Mr D.T. Hobbs, 77 The Gossamers, Garston, Watford.

Stoke Bruerne. Mr E. Burton, Rookery Farm, Rookery Lane, Stoke Bruerne, Towcester, Northants.

Stony Stratford WMC. Mr T.R. Valentine, 34 Malletts Close, Stony Stratford, Milton Keynes.

Tring Anglers. Mr J. Smith, 67 Lower Icknield Way, Marsworth, Nr Tring, Herts.

Watford Piscators. Mr N.F. Brandon, 25 Leaford Crescent, Watford, Herts.

Grand Union (Midlands)

Birmingham Anglers' Association
Mr F. Bayley, 40 Thorp Street, Birmingham.

British Legion Dorridge & Packwood Branch. Mr. V.J. Smith, Cover Point, 17 Earlswood Road, Dorridge, Solihull, West Midlands.

Charterhouse WMC. Mr H. Alford, 28 David Road, Coventry.

Coleshill & Dist. AS. Mr S.G. Smith, 38 Coventry Road, Coleshill, Birmingham.

Coventry & Dist. AA. Mr M. Williams, 134 Scots Lane, Coundon, Coventry.

Massey-Ferguson AS. Mr A. Wareham, c/o The Secretary, Massey-Ferguson Club, Banner Lane, Coventry.

Royal Leamington Spa AA. Mr E. Archer, 9 Southway, Leamington Spa, Warwickshire.

Warwick & Dist. AA. Mr L. Sargeant, 218 Warwick Road, Kenilworth, Warwickshire.

Wolseley Athletic & Social Club. Mr J.T. Gough, Drews Lane, Ward End, Birmingham.

Grand Union Branches:
Aylesbury Arm
A.C. Delco AS. Mr D.D. Billington, 26 Cheyne Close, Dunstable, Beds.
Tring Anglers. Mr J. Smith, 67 Lower Icknield Way, Marsworth, Nr Tring, Herts.

Leicester Branch
Coventry & Dist. AA. Mr M. Williams, 134 Scots Lane, Coundon, Coventry.
Leicester AC. Mr N.A. Barratt, 25 Crown Hills Rise, North Evington, Leicester.
Leicester AS. Mr N.W. Atkins, 31 Skelton Drive West, Knighton, Leicester.
Leicester & Dist. ASA. Mr J.C. Padmore, 181 Churchill Road, Thurmaston, Leicester.
Rugby Federation of Anglers. Mr J.M. Foster, 75 Francis Street, Stoneygate, Leicester.
Wigston AS. Mr A.J.R. Keleher, 20 Estoril Avenue, Wigston, Leicester.

Market Harborough Arm
Market Harborough & Dist. AS. Mr J.W. Ashton, 16 Connaught Road, Market Harborough.
Foxton Boat Services Limited. Foxted, Market Harborough.

Northampton Arm
Northampton Castle AC. Mr C.J. Howe, 137 Lutterworth Road, Northampton.

Grantham Canal

Cut to link Grantham with Nottingham, the Grantham Canal is now disused and neglected, but angling clubs with rights on the waterway are striving to get it restored. Very heavily weeded throughout much of its 30 miles, the Grantham takes a winding route passing by Woolsthorpe and Bottesford to join the Trent and Mersey Canal at Nottingham.

Gin-clear and quite shallow in places, it holds specimen fish of all varieties, but finding a clear spot in the weed can be difficult. As one association official put it 'The fishing is fabulous, but the weed problem is shocking, so you must know where to go. Tench to 4lb, bream to 7lb, pike to 30lb and carp to 18lb, are present as well as hefty perch and roach but they take some catching.'

At the Nottingham end the weed problem is nowhere near so severe but the fishing is equally as good, if not better. Chub to 5lb are taken from a section at the back of Nottingham Forest football ground as well as tench to 6lb. Roach, perch and carp are also present in fair numbers and, in a recent surveying operation, Severn–Trent W.A. netsmen captured an eel of nearly 10lb.

Licence – Anglian W.A. (Lincolnshire Division) from Grantham to Knipton. Severn–Trent W.A. elsewhere.

Where to Fish:
Grantham. Grantham AA have seven miles from Earlsfield Lane to the top lock at Woolsthorpe. Day tickets can be obtained from tackle shops in Grantham.
Woolsthorpe. Leicester & District AA control five miles from Woolsthorpe Wharfe to Redmile Bridge. Day tickets from tackle shops in Grantham or from the Rutland Arms, Woolsthorpe. Fishing between the top and bottom locks is also available on day tickets from the Rutland Arms.
Nottingham. Notts AA have a lengthy stretch on the outskirts of the town. Day tickets available. In the city itself Nottingham Harlequins AC lease the section between Lady Ham Bridge and Gamson Bridge, Radcliffe Road side.

Clubs and Secretaries:
Grantham AA. Mr S.C.E. Tearle, 8 Arnold Avenue, Grantham, Lincs.
Leicester & Dist. AA. Mr J.C. Padmore, 181 Churchill Road, Thurmaston, Leicester.
Notts AA. Mr L.E. Simpson, 92 Main St, Bulwell, Nottingham.
Nottingham Harlequin AC. Mr A.P. Hopkinson, 76 Bridgnorth Drive, Clifton Estate, Nottingham.

The Oxford Canal

The Oxford Canal, which links Coventry with Oxford is 91 miles in length. It runs south from its junction with the Coventry Canal at Hawkesbury to join the River Thames at Oxford. The Oxford Canal also links up with the Grand Union at Napton, Warwickshire, where for a short distance the two canals merge into one.

Influenced by the River Cherwell which runs into it at three points and merges with it for a considerable distance at Bletchington, the Oxford Canal has a pronounced flow below Banbury. It supports many running water species such as dace, chub and bleak besides the more usual roach, gudgeon, tench and carp. Perch, so rare in other waters, are quite prolific in places, no doubt due to a 20,000 stocking at Somerton by the Thames Water Authority.

One of the best canals in the country in its heyday, the Oxford is now like many other narrow and shallow waterways recovering after years of decline. Re-stocking by associations, the Severn–Trent and Thames Water Authorities and the British Waterways Board, has boosted sport considerably and some areas are now as good as they ever were.

At Coventry, near Hawkesbury Junction, roach to a pound are caught regularly, while at Anstey there are plenty of small bream. Below Brinklow fishing tends to be patchy but there is a good head of roach, plus perch which have tipped the scales at over 2lb. From Willoughby Wharfe towards Fenny Compton pleasure bags of bream and roach in excess of 20lb are not uncommon. Near Braunston big carp often set pulses racing and at the back of Shuckburgh village, bags of roach to 20lb, good perch to 1½lb and skimmer bream turn up regularly.

Below Fenny Compton big perch, roach, bream, tench and gudgeon are plentiful. Near Banbury warm water from the Alcan Works attracts carp, while roach and gudgeon plus odd chub are caught throughout the town waters. A hot spot is just above Grants Lock. Downstream of Twyford Bridge Coventry DAA injected 2,000 small tench, which are growing

The Oxford Canal at Bletchington, in summer

fast. From Nell Bridge onwards fishing is good as far as Somerton. Watch out for big perch as well as chub.

Below Lower Heyford towards Kirtlington, fishing is excellent and rated by many anglers as the cream of the Oxford Canal. Chub to 3lb, dace, bleak, perch, roach, gudgeon and bream are caught in good numbers. Heyford spinney is a notable roach area, while below Dashwood and Northbrooke Locks dace shoal in the compensation water. At Kirtlington, big hauls of roach are taken from the length at the back of the cement works. There are also plenty of gudgeon.

Three Pigeons Lock is another famous hot spot that has produced many excellent catches of roach, chub and dace. Bletchington is noted for hordes of small fish such as bleak, besides good roach. Below Kirtlington fishing is not as good as it used to be; in fact it can only be described as very patchy with odd pockets of fish.

Rod Licence – Thames W.A. Oxford to Fenny Compton. Severn–Trent W.A. (Severn Division) Fenny Compton to Coventry.

Where to Fish:
From Hawkesbury Junction to Bridge 27 near Anstey is controlled by Hawkesbury AC. Day tickets are available. Courtaulds AC have 1¼ miles (day ticket water) from Bridge 30 to just past Bridge 34. Rugby Federation then take over for 17 miles to Willoughby Wharfe – day tickets available. Coventry DAA take over from Rugby Federation at Bridge 83 and this length extends for 18 miles to Fenny Compton Wharfe Bridge 136 where day tickets may be obtained.

London AA have 1½ miles below the bridge that marks the boundary of the CDAA stretch. The Sphinx ACC (Coventry) then take over for a short length and the London Brick AC and Standard Recreation AC have short pieces farther on. Most of these club waters are open to visitors.

Banbury AA control from Copredy Lock to Bridge 160 near the Alcan works north of Banbury where day tickets are issued. Coventry DAA take over again at Bridge 160 to Nell Bridge 187 between Adderbury and Aynho, then Banbury AA have the next length from Bridge 187 to Lower Heyford wharf. Coventry DAA take over at the boundary of the Banbury stretch down to Thrupp and Kidlington Green Lock and from here North Oxford AS have the rights as far as the junction with the Thames.

Clubs and Secretaries:
Banbury & Dist. AC. Mr P.M. Handley, 8 Deene Close, Adderbury, Banbury, Oxon.
Courtaulds AC. Mr. J. Merry, British Celanese Ltd, P.O. Box 13, Little Heath, Coventry.
Coventry & Dist. AA. Mr M. Williams, 134 Scots Lane, Coundon, Coventry.
Hawkesbury AS. Mrs M. Woodward, 4 Tiveycourt Road, Coventry.
London AA. Mr H.J. Wilson, 183 Hoe Street, Walthamstow, London.

North Oxford AS. Mr A.H. Elsmore, 53 Plantation Road, Oxford.

Rugby Federation of Anglers. Mr J.M. Foster, 75 Francis Street, Stoneygate, Leicester.

The Sphinx Club, c/o Paradise Street, Coventry.

Standard Recreation Club, c/o The Pavilion, Tile Hall Lane, Coventry.

Oxford Canal – Stretton Arm Branch
Mr A. Rhead, The Railway Inn, Stretton under Fosse, Nr Rugby.

Rugby Federation of Anglers. Mr J.M. Foster, 75 Francis Street, Stoneygate, Leicester.

Shropshire Union

Constructed to link the Midlands, the North West, and Central Wales, the Shropshire Union Canal (and its four branches) forms one of the largest systems in the country. The main line stretches from Wolverhampton, in the West Midlands, to Ellesmere Port in Cheshire, where it enters the River Mersey. Two of its branches run into Wales, to Llangollen and Newtown (Montgomery Branch), one into Shropshire (near Prees) and the other, known as the Middlewich Branch, links with the Trent and Mersey Canal.

The Shropshire Union is a top-class canal in most anglers' books but if boats upset you steer clear of it at weekends in summer or you will have a nervous breakdown. It has been called 'the M6 on water' for the simple reason that the boat procession is never-ending. Mid-week is not so bad, or very early at weekends, but it is better to wait for autumn and winter. Then the boat traffic eases, the canal clears and double figure hauls are on the cards.

As on all other canals, sport along 'The Shroppy' as it is popularly known, deteriorated around 1967 but it has picked up again considerably over the past five years. In fact, there is a good head of roach, gudgeon, perch, bream, carp and eels, plus the occasional chub, in many sections.

Tactics for summer are usually floatfished small maggots – pinkies, squatts, anattos and gozzers – fished either close in or well across. When boat traffic is heavy, a light float leger close in pays dividends.

In winter 'The Shroppy' is a different canal. The flow is negligible and the water quite clear. Because the canal is elevated for much of its length, the temperature drops considerably, so the sheltered spots near bankside trees are often the best bet. Fish tend to congregate in these slightly warmer sections.

Winter catches are generally much better than summer with good roach coming to casters or bronze maggots presented well across or in the boat channel.

North of Market Drayton the most productive spots are the 'basins' or wider areas where bream tend to assemble. Tactics in these areas are light leger rigs swing-tipped well across with sour bran maggots or gozzers on the hook. Farther north, fishing varies from patchy to what can only be described as excellent. From Chester to Ellesmere Port, for instance, parts of 'The Shroppy' have shown a tremendous improvement in recent years with double-figure hauls of roach and bream taken in summer and through the winter, too.

Crucian carp and tench are also showing well. Notable is the Backford to Mollington section, a popular north-west contest venue that frequently produces big weights. Matches have been won with up to 14lb of bream, with class roach also figuring in the bulk of the catches.

Hempseed is a favourite summer and autumn bait in these parts and it seems to work almost anywhere with rod-tip and far-shelf tactics. Many matchmen use hemp with an 'on the drop' style, setting a single grain of seed to just touch bottom below a sensitive 'drinking straw' or loaded antenna float weighted with lead wire very near to the hook.

Rod Licence. The canal passes through three Water Authority areas – Severn–Trent, North West – Welsh National Water Development so it's best to enquire locally.

Where to Fish:
Autherley Junction, Wolverhampton, to Wheaton Aston on the Shropshire border, is controlled by Whitmore Reans CAA and the Provincial AA. Day tickets can be obtained on the towpath or from BWB Junction Office, Autherley or from the Whitmore Reans AA secretary. At Wheaton Aston, Hazeldine AA take over for 2½ miles from Wheaton Aston Locks to Bridge 23. This is member-only water. Private club water (Royal Exchange AS and Broomhill AC) adjoins the Hazeldine length and continues to High Onn Bridge where Izaak Walton (Stafford) take over.

Day tickets are available for the Stafford length which extends to Bridge 23 at Cowley only for the period June 16 to September 30. Hazeldine AA have more water from Bridge 23 to Cowley Tunnel (members only). Stoke City AA have lengths for members only between Gnosall and Grubb Street Bridge 41, and between Bridges 42 and 43 at Shebdon. The length between Bridges 41 and 42 is day-ticket water belonging to The Anchor Inn.

The section immediately above the Stoke water, at Woodseaves, starting at Bridge 44, belongs to Cleveland Road WMC (Wolverhampton) and is for members only. It extends to Bridge 45 at Knighton which marks the start of the Shropshire Union Canal AA water which runs to the end of the Main Line at Ellesmere Port. Day tickets are available for the whole of this length.

Clubs and Secretaries (Main Line):
Mr G.C. Cliff, Anchor Inn, Old Lea, High Offley, Woodseaves, Staffs.
Broomhill WMC. Secretary, Angling Section, Broomhill WMC, Cannock, Staffs.
Cleveland Road WMC. Secretary, Angling Section, Cleveland Road WMC, Cleveland Road, Wolverhampton.
Hazeldine AA. Mr J.W. Hazeldine, 8 Dudley Road, Sedgley, Dudley.
Izaak Walton (Stafford) AS. Mr R.S.B. Wilton, Brook House, Brook Lane, Brocton, Staffs.

Provincial AA. Mr W. Hunt, 11 Central Avenue, Bilston, W. Midlands.

Royal Exchange AS. Mr R. Brindley, 24 Scotia Road, Cannock, Staffs.

Shropshire Union Canal AA. Mr R. Brown, 10 Dale Road, Golborne, Lancs.

Stoke City & Dist. AA. Mr P. Johansen, 31 East Crescent, Sneyd Green, Stoke-on-Trent.

Llangollen Branch

Running from Harlaston Junction above Nantwich, Cheshire, through Ellesmere, Salop and Chirk, the Llangollen Branch is a picturesque waterway which offers excellent fishing in parts. Weed is a problem in some sections but, by choosing his spot, the pleasure angler can find quality bream, roach, perch, pike and gudgeon.

Where to Fish: .

Apart from a length between Bridge 55 and Bridge 58 near Ellesmere, which is reserved for members of Ellesmere AC, the whole of the canal is controlled by the Shropshire Union AA which offers day-ticket facilities.

Clubs and Secretaries:

Ellesmere AC. Mr L. Walton, 51 Scotland Street, Ellesmere, Salop.

Shropshire Union Canal AA. Mr R. Brown, 10 Dale Road, Golborne, Lancs.

Middlewich Branch

This canal connects the Shropshire Union with the Trent and Mersey and runs for 10 miles from Barbridge Junction, north of Nantwich, to Middlewich. Fishing rights for the whole length are held by the Shropshire Union AA and again day tickets are available.

Clubs and Secretaries:

Shropshire Union Canal AA. Mr R. Brown, 10 Dale Road, Golborne, Lancs.

Montgomery Branch
This scenic canal leaves the Llangollen Branch at Franklin, near Ellesmere, and runs through Llanymynech, Welshpool and on to Newtown in mid Wales. De-watered in parts, overgrown with weed and silted up in others, this canal nevertheless produces good catches of bream and roach in some sections.

Where to Fish:
Associations with rights reserve fishing for members only but day-ticket facilities are available on the Cammell Laird AC stretch at Abermule, the Dolphin Inn water at Llanymynech, and a short length at Welshpool.

Clubs and Secretaries:
Argae Hall AC. Mr J. Woodcock, 6 Maes Beuno, Berriew, Welshpool.
Brunswick AC. Mr A. Williams, 218 Muirhead Avenue, Liverpool.
Cammell Laird's Sports Club AS. Mr F.S. Duckers, 2 Ivy Avenue, Brackenwood, Bebington, Wirral.
Hazeldine AA. Mr J.W. Hazeldine, 8 Dudley Road, Sedgley, Dudley.
Provincial AA. Mr W. Hunt, 11 Central Avenue, Bilston, West Midlands.
Royal Exchange AS. Mr Brindley, 24 Scotia Road, Cannock.
Stafford I.W. AA. Mr R.S.B. Wilton, Brook House, Brook Lane, Brocton, Staffs.
Shropshire Union CAA. Mr R. Brown, 10 Dale Road, Golborne, Lancs.
Stoke City & DAA. Mr P. Johansen, 31 East Crescent, Sneyd Green, Stoke-on-Trent.
Whitmore Reans CAA. Mr R.H. Hughes, Star Chambers, Princes Square, Wolverhampton.

Prees Branch
This short waterway, which runs from near Ellesmere to Prees, Shropshire, has been neglected but still produces fish.

Fishing along the whole length is controlled by the Shropshire Union Canal AA which offers day-ticket facilities; secretary Mr R. Brown, 10 Dale Road, Golborne, Lancs.

Staffordshire and Worcester Canal

Constructed to link the Trent and Mersey and the North West system with the River Severn, the Staffs–Worcester runs from Great Haywood near Stafford through Stafford, Wolverhampton and Kidderminster to join the River Severn at Stourport. It also connects with the Shropshire Union at Autherley Junction, Wolverhampton.

A popular West Midland contest venue, the Staffs–Worcester Canal has shown a tremendous improvement in recent years. Practically the whole of the canal produces reasonable sport and although gudgeon are the predominant species, roach, carp, perch, bream and tench are also caught in many sections. Generally, this canal can be described as a 'small fish water'. The gudgeon often run to forty-five to the pound and any fish over the 1lb mark is unusual.

The exception is the Milford section, near Stafford, which holds a good head of tench averaging between two and three pounds. These fish provide excellent summer fishing and double figure bags are quite common even in matches. Elsewhere, hauls of mixed catches around the 3lb mark are usually enough to win contests, although early morning and late evening pleasure anglers often catch up to 10lb bags of roach on hempseed or casters. Wolverley, near Kidderminster, is noted for its roach which feed freely in winter and summer when conditions are quiet.

Rod Licence – Severn–Trent W.A.

Where to Fish:
The Birmingham Anglers' Association (members only but membership open to anyone) control fishing from Stourport to Swindon, near Wolverhampton, apart from a short length

at Stewponey which is leased by Kinver Freeliners AC. From the BAA boundary at Botterham Locks to Wightwick Locks is Whitmore Reans CAA water where day tickets can be obtained in advance from the secretary. From Wolverhampton to Penkridge the canal is shared by a number of clubs, most of which issue day tickets or allow contest bookings. Whitmore Reans CAA have another 4½ miles at Penkridge which extends from the Boat Inn, in the town, to Bridge 94 towards Stafford. Izaak Walton (Stafford) AA then take over a long stretch which runs to the Potteries AS water near the junction at Great Haywood.

Clubs and Secretaries:
Birmingham AA. Mr F. Bayley, 40 Thorp Street, Birmingham.
Blackfords Progressive AS. Mr C. Williams, 4 Johns Lane, Great Wyrley, Walsall, West Midlands.
Broomhill AS. Mr R. Brindley, 24 Scotia Road, Cannock, Staffs.
Essington WMC. Mr J. Bradburn, 54 Upper Sneyd Road, Essington, Wolverhampton.
Goodyear AS. Mr M.K. Bethel, 47 Brook Close, The Woodlands, Coven, Wolverhampton.
Izaak Walton (Stafford) AA. Mr R.S.B. Wilton, Brook House, Brook Lane, Brocton, Staffs.
M.C. Welded Fabrications AS. Mr K. Mantle, Unit 12, Blakenhall Industrial Estate, Sunbeam Street, Wolverhampton.
Newey (Tipton) AC. Mr E.A. Icke, 35 Waterfield Close, Tipton, West Midlands.
Potteries AS. Mr W. Bowers, 101 Broadway, Meir, Stoke-on-Trent.
Provincial AA. Mr W. Hunt, 11 Central Avenue, Bilston, West Midlands.
Richard Ross AC. Mr J. Galloway, 16 Whitston Avenue, Ashmore Park Estate, Wednesfield, Wolverhampton.
Ernest Thomas (Walsall) Ltd. Old Birchills Wharf, Walsall.
Whitmore Reans CAA. Mr R.H. Hughes, Princes Square, Wolverhampton.

Stourbridge and Dudley Canals

These canals form a loop on the outskirts of the Black Country joining the Staffs–Worcester at Stourton Junction near Stourbridge and the Birmingham Canal near Tipton. Polluted to some extent, particularly where they run through industrial districts, the canals are reputed to hold carp and tench, plus a good head of roach. The best fishing is to be had along the southernmost lengths where the waterway flows through country or rural areas but, according to regular visitors, a certain amount of searching is necessary to contact the shoals.

Licence – Severn–Trent W.A.

Where to Fish:
Kidderminster DAA control 1½ miles between Stewponey and Stourbridge. No day tickets are issued but honorary membership cards are available to anyone.
Dudley. Sandwell Anglers Council have two miles between Windmill End and Garretts Lane Bridge. which is free to anyone willing to submit a report on the quality of the fishing.

Clubs and Secretaries:
Kidderminster DAA. Mr K.D. Powell, Little House, Woodstow, Lindridge, Nr Tenbury Wells, Worcs.
Sandwell Anglers Council. Mr K. Duffell, Grenville Drive, Smethwick, Warley, West Midlands.
Warley Rag AC. Mr A.J. Smallwood, 20 Lansbury Road, Cradley Heath, Warley, West Midlands.

Stratford-on-Avon Canal

Built to link Birmingham with the River Avon at Stratford, this canal starts from a junction with the Worcester–Birmingham at Kings Norton and runs for twenty-two miles to join the River Avon at Stratford. It also links up with the Grand Union at Kingswood Junction. On leaving the suburbs of Birmingham, the Stratford canal passes through quiet and pleasant Warwickshire countryside which makes it a popular haunt for Birmingham anglers.

Once famous for big hauls of bream, the Stratford has been in the doldrums in recent years, so much so that Birmingham AA have stopped using it for big canal contests. Until around 1976 it held a fair head of small roach and bream, plus larger bream in odd pockets, and occasional tench, perch and carp. These days fishing has become very patchy and while pleasure anglers frequently report double-figure bags, contest weights are very poor and there are usually many dry nets.

Rod Licence – Severn–Trent W.A.

Where to Fish:
Birmingham Anglers' Association control the whole of the fishing from Birmingham to Stratford. No day tickets are issued but the association is open to all (40 Thorp Street, Birmingham B5 4AU).

Trent and Mersey Canal

Cut to link the River Mersey and the River Trent, the Trent and Mersey connects so many other canal systems that it was once known simply as 'The Grand Trunk'. Commencing at Preston Brook Junction on the Bridgewater Canal, it runs across Cheshire, through Middlewich, and on to the Potteries passing almost through the centre of this great industrial area. From Stoke-on-Trent the canal runs through Trentham and Stone then skirts Stafford to join the Staffs–Worcester at Great Haywood. Leaving Great Haywood it passes through Rugeley and Armitage and down to Fradley Junction, near Lichfield, where it connects with the Coventry Canal. From Fradley it makes a right angle turn to run north through Alrewas and on to Burton where it terminates at its junction with the River Trent.

The Trent and Mersey has fished really well in parts over the past few years, with excellent contest results and big pleasure catches. Re-stocking by clubs and associations, plus a lot of work done by British Waterways Board and the natural return of some species after a near wipe-out in the mid sixties, have contributed in the restoration of the Trent and Mersey's great reputation as a fishery.

But for the almost endless cavalcade of pleasure craft during the summer, sport would be better now than it has ever been on some lengths. That's the opinion of Peter Johansen, secretary of Stoke City AS, a club which has leased several miles near Stafford for many years. After spending £3,000 on re-stocking, Stoke City members are enjoying excellent sport with roach, bream, a few chub, as well as tench and carp. Also, to please the match angler, there's a large head of gudgeon.

This story can be repeated for dozens of other sections and, after speaking to a number of club representatives, it is clear that this canal is bursting with fish life. Some of the best areas at present lie between Burton and Rugeley. Here, roach, perch, gudgeon, small carp, and occasional bream produce memorable pleasure bags and eye-catching match weights around the 7lb mark.

Contests are always a good barometer of a canal's potential and it is interesting to note that, given reasonable conditions, there are seldom any dry nets on the Trent and Mersey. Another good section worth a mention lies between Colwich Lock and Wolseley Bridge, north of Rugeley. British Waterways Board stocked this piece in 1972 and the transplanted mirror carp, bream, and roach have thrived in flowing water of excellent quality.

Licence – North West W.A. from Kidsgrove to Preston Brook
Severn–Trent W.A. elsewhere

Where to Fish:
British Waterways Board control certain sections, notably Fradley, near Lichfield, and Colwich near Stafford, day tickets for which can be purchased from patrolling bailiffs. Full details of BWB waters, match bookings etc. can be

obtained from the Amenity Officer, BWB, Chester Road, Nantwich, Cheshire.

Above and around Burton the canal is mostly controlled by small clubs. Burton Mutual AA lease the length between Clay Mills and Wychnor, Bridges 28 to 42. Day tickets are issued through the association Match Section. Bass Worthington AC have 1½ miles from Tatenhill Lane, Branston, to the allotments at Shobnall, which is reserved for members.

Alrewas AC have a lengthy stretch that extends from Trent Lock, Alrewas, to Hunts Lock above Fradley Junction. Day tickets are available through the secretary.

From Kings Bromley to Armitage, Walsall DAS own outright five miles of the canal from Wood End to Handsacre. Day and seasonal permits through the secretary.

Rugeley and Brereton AS take over at the boundary of the Walsall DAS stretch for seven miles as far as Wolseley Bridge, north of Rugeley. No day tickets, but contests and block bookings through the secretary. Wolseley Bridge to Colwich Lock is controlled by BWB, day tickets on the towpath from patrolling bailiffs.

British Rail Staff Association (Stoke Branch) AS lease, in conjunction with Izaak Walton (Stafford) AA, the section between Great Haywood Lock and Ingestre Bridge (78). This is member-only water and no permits are issued. Fenton and District AS take over at Meaford Lock as far as Whieldon Road Bridge, Fenton, Stoke-on-Trent, a distance of seven miles. No day tickets but the matter is under consideration, so apply to the secretary.

Stoke City & District AA have the fishing from Aston, near Stone, to Ingestre Lock, a length of five miles. No day tickets, but membership is open. Stone & District AS lease 2¾ miles between Aston Lock and Meaford Lock and day tickets can be obtained from the secretary.

At Stoke, Middleport WMC AC control a length between Lord Street Bridge, Etruria, and Hardcastle Tunnel. No day tickets but season permits are issued through the secretary.

At Sandbach, Royal British Legion (Middlewitch) AS have 2½ miles from Rookery Bridge, No. 159, to Booth Lane

Locks. Members only are allowed to fish this section. Cheshire AA control the fishing from Rode Heath Bridge (No. 141) to Rookery Bridge (No. 159), a distance of five miles. Again, this is for members only.

At Middlewich, Cheshire AA have more fishing between Booth Lane Locks and the junction with the Shropshire Union Canal. This two-mile section is for members only. From Middlewich to Preston Brook, where the canal terminates, is controlled by Northwich AA. Day tickets available on the towpath.

Clubs and Secretaries:

BWB day tickets are available for certain sections. Details, and contest bookings, through Mr J.G. Taylor, Information and Booking Assistant, BWB, Basin End, Chester Road, Nantwich, Cheshire.

Alrewas AC. Mr A.R. Booth, 3 Ivanhoe Road, Lichfield, Staffs.

Bass Worthington AC. c/o Bass Worthington Limited, Burton-on-Trent, Staffs.

British Rail Staff Association AS. Mr E. Greasley, 4 Winton Square, Stoke-on-Trent, Staffs.

Burton Mutual AA. Mr D.J. Clarke, 7 Denton Rise, Burton-on-Trent.

Cheshire AA. Mr F.R. James, 34 Sweetbriar Crescent, Crewe.

Derby AA, Mr T. Hickton, 7 Crecy Close, Derby.

Derby Railway Institute FC. Mr K. Ottewell, 65 Leytonstone Drive, Mackworth, Derby.

Fenton & District AS. Mr A.R. Burgess, 77 Drubbery Lane, Longton, Stoke-on-Trent.

Middleport WMC. Mr G. James, 70 Gordon Street, Burslem, Stoke-on-Trent.

North Staffs. AA. Mr C. Moore, 38 Debenham Crescent, Stoke-on-Trent.

Northwich AA. Mr F.E. Edwards, 19 Bowden Drive, Northwich, Cheshire.

Royal British Legion (Middlewich) AC. Mr G. Ashmore, 22 Ashfield Street, Middlewich, Cheshire.

Rugeley & Brereton AS. Mr D. Mellor, 56 Upper Lodge Road, Armitage, Staffs.

Stoke City & District AA. Mr P. Johansen, 31 East Crescent, Sneyd Green, Stoke-on-Trent.

Stone and District AS. Mr A.J. Lockley, 7 Queen Street, Stone, Staffs.

Trent and Mersey Canal AA. Mr F. Egerton, 19 Bowden Drive, Northwich, Cheshire.

Walsall DAS. Mr A. Clarke, 18 Roche Road, Mossley Estate, Bloxwich, Walsall, West Midlands.

Caldon Branch:
This seventeen-mile long branch of the Trent and Mersey runs from Etruria, north of Stoke-on-Trent, to Froghall, Staffs. Clear, and with quite a strong flow, this canal offers reasonable sport in places with roach, gudgeon, carp, bream and tench, but the best fishing is undoubtedly to be had towards Leek.

Licence – Severn–Trent W.A.

Where to Fish:
Burslem Izaak Walton AS lease a section between Bullers Works, Milton, and Hazelhurst Junction above Endon. Day tickets are available from the secretary or bailiffs at Stockton Brook, Norton Green, and Park Lane, Endon. Shelton Private AC take over at Hazelhurst Locks to Cheddleton Road Bridge, a distance of 1¾ miles. No day tickets at present but possibilities in the future. Leek and Moorlands control six miles from Cheddleton Road Bridge to Froghall Basin. Day tickets here are available in advance only to bona fide visitors to the area.

Clubs and Secretaries:
Burslem Izaak Walton AS. Mr R.W. Burdon, 77 Albany Road, Harpfields, Stoke-on-Trent, Staffs.

Leek and Moorlands WMC AC. Mr E. Salt, 4 Union Street, Leek, Staffs.

North Staffs. AA. Mr C. Moore, 38 Debenham Crescent, Bucknall, Stoke-on-Trent.

Shelton Private AC. Mr R. Horwell, 17 Lionel Grove, Harpfields, Stoke-on-Trent.

WHERE TO FISH: SOUTH AND WEST

Basingstoke Canal

Cut to link Basingstoke, in Hampshire, with the River Wey in Surrey, this canal runs from Weybridge via Odiham to Basingstoke, a distance of 40 miles.

Neglected and disused for many years, it is only inches deep, or has completely dried up in places. But good news for anglers is that it is being restored from end to end. Surrey and Hampshire County Councils are behind the scheme and an eight-mile length near Odiham has already been dredged, refilled and stocked with fish. This section is fishing well, too, by all accounts, so well in fact that the first open contest for 12 years is being held in 1979.

One length of the Basingstoke that has always provided excellent sport is at Mytchett. Here the canal widens into a lake and, with 12 feet of water at their feet along the towpath, anglers take good catches of bream, tench, roach and other species. Farnborough anglers rate this length as one of the best fisheries in the south.

Licence – Southern W.A.

Where to Fish:
The Basingstoke Canal Amalgamation of Anglers, comprising Hampshire and Surrey clubs, control the whole of the fishing. Day tickets can be obtained on the towpath.

Clubs and Secretaries:
Basingstoke Canal AA. Mr M. Hatcher, 80 Hillview Court, Guildford Road, Woking.

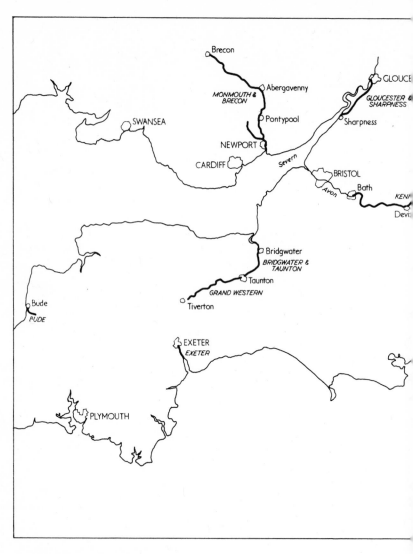

Canals of the South and South West

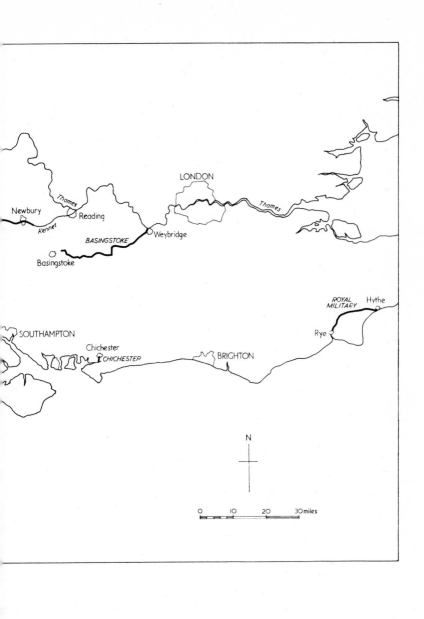

Newbury
Thames
Reading
Kennet
BASINGSTOKE
Weybridge
Basingstoke

LONDON
Thames

ROYAL
MILITARY
Hythe
Rye

SOUTHAMPTON
Chichester
CHICHESTER
BRIGHTON

N

0   10   20   30 miles

Bridgwater and Taunton Canal

This canal runs from Taunton to Bridgwater, linking the River Tone with the River Parrett. Extremely clear and very weedy in parts, the canal has a constant flow towards Bridgwater that influences tactics and methods.

Roach, rudd, tench, bream and pike are the main species and they often reach specimen proportions. Big fish reported in the last three years include rudd to 2¾lb, roach to 2lb 11oz, tench over 5lb and bream to 5½lb. Bronze maggots, casters and breadflake are the most popular baits but many tench are taken on worms. Past records from the water reveal rudd of 3lb 12oz, roach 2lb 14oz, pike 27lb 3½oz and chub 5lb 2oz.

Licence – Wessex W.A.

Where to Fish:
The whole of the canal can be fished on day tickets, available from either Bridgwater AA or Taunton AA outlets such as local tackle dealers.
Bridgwater AA have the rights from Bridgwater Docks to Durston, and Taunton AA from Durston to Taunton.

Clubs and Secretaries:
Bridgwater AA. Mr B. Valentine-Slack, 6 Toll House Road, Cannington, Somerset.
Taunton AA. Mr H. R. King, 13 Radlett Close, Taunton, Somerset.

An angler swings in a small fish taken from the Taunton–Bridgwater Canal, a popular winter venue

Bude Canal

A canalised river, the Bude Canal flows from the junction of the Rivers Stratt and Neet into Bude Bay, a distance of approximately three miles. With and average depth of four to five feet and a steady current, it offers good summer fishing with carp and tench, though most varieties of coarse fish are also caught. The most popular section is in Bude itself, where holiday visitors can fish only a few yards from the beach.

Licence – South West W.A.

Where to Fish:
Bude AA control the whole of the fishing. Day tickets can be obtained at the waterside.

Clubs and Secretaries:
Bude AA. Mr D. Allen, 10 Fairholme Road, Bude, Cornwall.

Chichester Canal

Only four miles in length, the canal runs from the Basin in the centre of Chichester through Hunston and Donnington to join an arm of the Chichester Harbour estuary, below Birdham.

Somewhat neglected in the past, this canal is being restored, and the first mile from Chichester to Donnington has been dredged. Unfortunately, the dredging has increased an already extensive weed problem. The fish population consists of a good head of wild carp, roach, bream and perch, plus a few rudd, and some pike and eels. The carp (which run to just short of double-figures) give good sport once located, which can sometimes be difficult because of the weed. The canal is mainly fished by individuals and is unsuitable for contests.

Licence – South West W.A.

Where to Fish:
Fishing throughout is controlled by the Chichester Canal Anglers' Association, a consortium of clubs. Day tickets for

the whole of the canal can be obtained from local tackle dealers or the village store at Donnington.

Clubs and Secretaries:
Chichester Canal AA. Mr A. W. Pascoe, Wesley Grove, Copnor, Portsmouth, Hants.

Exeter Canal

This 5½-mile long canal, begun in 1564–6, runs from Exeter to Turf near Powderham where it enters the sea. Wide and deep, (it has an average width of 30 yards and a depth of 11 to 12 feet) it formerly carried coasters into Exeter but they ceased plying a few years ago.

Holding a large variety of coarse fish, the Exeter Canal has yielded many outstanding catches over the years, although since the boat traffic has stopped, sport has deteriorated somewhat. This is because conditions have changed. The water has become much clearer and weedier, thus providing a lot of natural food. Present stocks are good and include roach, tench, bream, carp, perch, pike and dace. The latter species have entered the canal from the River Exe, to which it is connected, and they run to a good size. Rudd are also much in evidence, which is not surprising since Exeter AA, who control the fishing, introduced 20,000, along with some carp, a few years ago. More re-stocking was carried out in 1978. Favourite tactics for all species is either floatfishing or legering well across with caster or bronze maggots.

Licence – South West W.A.

Where to Fish:
Exeter AA lease the rights on both banks for the whole of the canal. Day or weekly permits are obtainable from local tackle dealers or The Bridge Café, Countess Wear, Exeter.

Clubs and Secretaries:
Exeter & District AA. Mr D. L. Beaven, 46 Hatherleigh Road, Exeter.

A stretch of the Gloucester Canal – a waterway still used by large barges and tankers

The Gloucester and Sharpness Canal

A commercial ship canal, which by-passes an unnavigable reach of the lower Severn below Gloucester, the 16-mile long Gloucester Canal re-enters the tidal Severn below a huge sea-lock at Sharpness. With a mid-channel depth of around 13 feet and a width that varies between 25 and 50 yards, the canal is a big water that invites many styles to explore the swims in full. Unpredictable, the canal nevertheless produces excellent catches of roach, chub and bream in summer and winter. Odd big carp, tench, dace, eels and perch also turn up regularly at most venues.

The water is heavily match-fished at the Hempstead, Gloucester end, a length which is generally recognised as the best on the canal. Here there are 250 permanent pegs which run from Hempstead Bridge to midway between Rea Bridge and the Pilot Inn. Over the years, chub, roach and bream have all played their part in winning catches, and the methods evolved by leading match anglers to catch these species are generally regarded as the best for the whole canal.

Most fish are caught on the near and far shelves where the depth is around four feet, or on the steep slopes running away from the shelves towards mid-channel. The shelves are about six feet wide and then the bed drops to 11 feet about a rod and a half out. The chub, which run to 3lb, invariably hug the far bank and the local experts are adept at fishing right across, either with a waggler or a light leger rig. Loose feeding maggots or casters is an important part of this method, so a catapult is essential.

Because of its great width the canal invariably catches the wind. In fact the slightest breeze is enough to build up a pull on the surface. The answer to this is a 2½ swan-shot bodied waggler, set to drag the bottom and normally shotted with a number 8 a foot from the hook, two number 4s spread equally above, and the rest locking the float. Because the chub are nervous and finicky, fine terminal tackle is necessary: 1lb bottoms and small hooks (22s, 20s and 18s) with a 1½lb reel line is the normal rig and, because there is no weed, this set-up will land anything – even double-figure carp.

When the wind is very strong, or on very cold days, the leger comes into its own, but a light sliding link is enough to hold bottom. Three swan shot are usually adequate unless there is a very strong pull.

Bream are now appearing in large numbers at Hempstead and they are a nice sample, running to 1¾lb. These fish are well spread in the area, almost at every peg. Maggot is the top bait for bream until October. Some groundbait is essential but should be kept to a minimum, say five pints for five hours, and mix in plenty of squatts. Obviously, the lead is the best method for bream but it is always worth trying the waggler to attract the odd fish that wants a moving bait.

Roach fishing on the Gloucester Canal is unpredictable. Although there is a large head of class fish, conditions have to be just right to induce them to feed. On the right day you can catch them under the rod end on virtually any bait. Hempseed and tares fished this way, by individual anglers, have accounted for some marvellous bags. But these baits are a long-odds gamble in matches. Casters and maggots, with a small amount of hempseed as feed, are more consistent. When seeking roach it is important to find the contour of the near-side shelf and concentrate on this spot. The float for this technique is a matter of choice. A stick is effective if the pull is not too great, and bird quills are also popular patterns.

Rod Licence: Severn–Trent W.A.

Where to Fish:
Fishing is available on its 16-mile length by buying a yearly or day permit from Gloucester tackle shops or from bridge keepers. The Castle length is good for roach and bream each side of the bridge. The junction with the Stroud Canal is a good chub area, with some roach, and the latter species is also starting to return in the lengths below Frampton. Splatt Bridge is improving, especially for winter roach: try the bay and the pegs immediately below. From Slimbridge to Purton the species are the same, but there are fewer of them until towards the docks where the population begins to build up.

Access can be gained from any of the 12 road bridges between Hempstead, near Gloucester, and Purton, near Sharpness. Reservations for club contests should be made through the British Waterways Board Amenity Services Supervisor (SW), Dock Office, Gloucester (Gloucester 25524).

Grand Western Canal

One of the few canals in the West Country, the 11-mile long waterway was intended to run from Tiverton to the Taunton–Bridgwater Canal. But, for various reasons, it was never completed and terminates at Burlescombe.

Only two to 2½ feet deep, the canal is very weedy along the whole of its length though this is cut regularly at the Tiverton end in the summer months to allow the passage of a large pleasure barge.

Generally considered a summer fishery, the water holds a good head of tench, which provide good sport until October time. Roach (a 2lb 2oz specimen was caught a few years ago), rudd, and bream are also much in evidence. The latter species was introduced by the local angling associations in the Tiverton area and they have spread as far as Sampford Peverell, a section noted for its big pike. In fact, the Grand Western is famous for its big pike, skeletons of which can be seen in Tiverton Museum. The best pike taken in recent years was a 23-pounder in 1978, but many double-figure fish have been recorded over the last few years. The most popular spot on the canal is Tiverton Basin in the town.

Licence – South West W.A.

Where to Fish:
Tiverton AS lease the fishing rights for the whole canal from Devon County Council. Day tickets are obtainable in advance from all tackle shops in the area, Devon County Council Offices, Exeter, and the Post Office, Sampford Peverell.

The Kennet and Avon Canal

With water of chalk-stream quality – it is fed by springs and the River Kennet which forms part of the length – the Kennet and Avon is a canal in a class of its own. Renowned for its large head of all species (which often attain specimen proportions) this 87-mile-long waterway connects to the River Thames at Reading and with the Bristol Avon at Bath.

Its constant flow in many sections often calls for light leger river-style tactics to catch big bream up to 10lb, double-figure carp and pike, roach over 2lb, plus quality dace, tench, rudd, chub and even barbel. At present much of the canal is unnavigable, which makes it an anglers' paradise, but there are plans afoot to restore the whole of its length to accommodate pleasure craft.

From Reading to Newbury the canal is largely the River Kennet with canalised lengths. Barbel are the predominant species, with roach, chub and dace also figuring in catches.

A stretch of the Kennet and Avon Canal at Hungerford

Fine tackle is a must on this length, which is heavily fished.
Legering is the top method along the faster flowing sections,
with luncheon meat an excellent bait for barbel.

Newbury to Hungerford produces plenty of heavy roach
plus sizeable bream and occasional big pike. The Hungerford
to Pewsey length is rated one of the best sections of the canal
with bream, tench, roach, rudd, perch, pike and carp running
to specimen proportions. Of special note is the area around
the Crofton Pumphouse where roach over 2lb, bream to 9lb
and tench over 7lb are not uncommon.

Pewsey to Wilcot is noted for big catches of bream as well
as other species. Tench can be caught at most spots and
perch, too, offer good sport. Fishing can be patchy from
Wilcot to Staverton and there has been some pollution in
recent years. Nevertheless, bream, tench and roach are
caught at many venues.

Staverton to Claverton is noted for its tench catches, especially at Limpley Stoke where this species thrives in the weedy surroundings. Big bream to 9lb are a feature of the Claverton to Bath length where tench and roach are also taken in large numbers. At Bathampton, tench are the predominant fish in the summer months, with bags around the 100lb not unknown. Towards Bath the canal has been developed by local associations and produces excellent catches of carp to 6lb, tench to 4lb, plus plenty of quality roach.

Rod Licence – Thames W.A. Reading to Wootton Bassett, Wessex W.A. Wootton Bassett to Bath.

Where to Fish:
Reading to Newbury. Thatcham AA and Reading DAA control 23 miles for members only. Day tickets for left-bank section at Aldermaston available at the waterside.
Sulhampstead. Tickets at the waterside for ¾ mile.

Thatcham. Tickets in advance from local tackleists, for two miles.

Newbury and District AA control the canal from Newbury to above Hungerford. No day tickets are issued and membership is limited to residents living within a 12-mile radius of Newbury. The Hungerford Canal AA have 2½ miles near Hungerford for which day tickets are issued. Applications should be made to Mr Paul Good, Ironmonger, High Street, Hungerford.

Marlborough AC lease a long length between Hungerford and Pewsey, some of which is available on day tickets. These can be had from Marlborough Pet Shop, 106 High Street, Marlborough; Mr John Last, Hillbarn House Cottage, Great Bedwyn, or Mr Fribbance, Crofton Railway Crossing Cottage.

A picturesque stretch of the heavily fished Kennet and Avon Canal at Devizes

Pewsey AA control a lengthy stretch from Lady's Bridge, Wilcot, to Milkhouse Water, Pewsey, for which day tickets are available. Apply (in advance) to the tackle shop, Pewsey or to the Pewsey AA secretary.

Between Wilcot and Staverton, Devizes AA have the rights for 15 miles from Lady's Bridge to Semington Bridge, Devizes, for which day tickets can be obtained in advance from local tackleists or The Barge Inn, Seend, and The Barge Inn, Honeystreet. The association is open to anyone.

Between Staverton and Claverton, Bristol and West of England Federation of Anglers control the fishing from Limpley Stoke Aqueduct to Dundas Aqueduct. No day permits are issued but the association is open to affiliation.

Bathampton AA control most of Claverton to Bath length and, though no day permits are available, the association is open to anyone.

Monmouth and Brecon Canal

Built to link Brecon with Newport and the sea, the Monmouth and Brecon Canal follows the course of the River Usk in places and passes through Tal-y-bont, Crickhowell, Abergavenny and Pontypool on its way to Newport, Gwent. An arm also runs from Newport to Crumlin.

Somewhat neglected and very weedy in parts, the canal holds roach, carp, tench, bream, and rudd plus a few trout and dace in certain sections. Clubs with leases are attempting to improve the fishing by re-stocking and dredging. Pontypool AA, in conjunction with the Pontypool Canal Society, have made some progress in this respect and, according to some of the catches made on their stretches in 1978 (40lb bags of carp) the future of the water looks promising.

Many lengths in the middle reaches are rarely fished except by casual anglers, so the potential of a large proportion of the canal is an unknown quantity.

Licence – Welsh National W.D.A.
(Usk Division).

Where to Fish:

British Steel Corporation AS have four miles from Bridge 132, Llangatock to Crickhowell. Season permits available from the secretary.

At Mamhilad Pontllanfraith AS lease three quarters of a mile between Bridges 58 and 62. Day tickets from the secretary.

Pontypool AA control one mile with boundaries at the Jockey Bridge and Bridge 57. Day tickets from Typoeth Stores, near Jockey Bridge, and Sports Shop, Pontypool.

Crumlin Arm (Newport to Risca): tickets on towpath or from tackleist in Risca.

Royal Military Canal

Originally dug as part of a defence line against possible invasion during the Napoleonic Wars, the Royal Military was intended to carry army supplies to fortifications along the Kent and Sussex coast. Running from Hythe to Rye, the waterway is over 20 miles long and acts as a drainage system to relieve flooding in the surrounding area.

With easy access along the whole of its length, the canal is a popular fishery and scene of many big contests. Main species are roach, bream and tench with occasional perch, carp, rudd, gudgeon and pike. Tench provide good sport in summer with the best specimens running up to 6lb in the deeper stretches at the opposite ends of the canal. From Hythe to Aldergate, for instance, there are swims up to eight feet deep which are renowned for tench and some fair bream up to 4lb. Roach are fairly well spread in the area.

Aldergate to Giggers Green is the haunt of several good bream shoals; roach and perch are also taken in fair numbers. Giggers Green to Bilsington is a favourite stretch for roach, although weed can be a problem.

Bilsington to Kenardington has been recently dredged, which has cured the weed problem, but whether the roach, perch and gudgeon, which formerly gave good sport, will still be around when the water settles is questionable. Kenardington to Appledore has produced a few carp in recent years but roach, bream, perch, rudd and tench are the main species. Appledore to Iden Lock is overgrown with weed in parts but tench, bream and roach are taken in good numbers from the clearer stretches.

Recently the Royal Military has hit the headlines with some monster carp. The biggest so far, which tipped the scales at 32lb, fell to Ashford (Kent) specimen hunter Bill Phillips, who has studied the canal carp population for ten years. A plastics technologist, Bill caught seven over 20lb in 1978 and has many more in the high teens to his credit. His previous best was a 25-pounder landed in 1974. Most of these carp have come from the Iden Lock–West Hythe stretch to high protein baits.

Licence – Southern W.A.

Where to Fish:
Ashford AS control the whole of the fishing except for a short length at Seabrook. Day tickets can be obtained from local tackleists; The Canal Cottage, Iden Lock; Red Lion and Swan Hotels, Appledore; Monument Garage, Bilsington and Hurst Poultry Farm, Giggers Green.

Appendix

Water Authorities Issuing Licences

Anglian Water Authority (AWA)
Regional Licence on an annual or seven-day basis for whole area.
Divisional Licences on a similar basis.
Division 1 Lincolnshire
Division 2 Welland and Nene catchment area
Division 3 Great Ouse
Division 4 Norfolk and Suffolk
Division 5 Essex

Northumbrian Water Authority (NWA)
Annual freshwater licence issued.

North West Water Authority (NWWA)
Annual and seven-day licences available for freshwater fish and eels.
Separate annual licences available for former Mersey and Weaver
River Authority. Temporary group licence for contests of ten or
more anglers available in advance.

Severn–Trent Water Authority (STWA)
Divisional licence for whole region: 28-day or annual. Regional for
either Severn or Trent catchments: 28-day or annual.

Southern Water Authority (SWA)
Licence for freshwater fish and eels available on 14-day or annual
basis.

South West Water Authority (SWWA)
Licence for freshwater fish and eels on annual basis.

Thames Water Authority (TWA)
Licence including all species available on annual, 28-day or one-day
basis.

Welsh National Water Development Authority (WNWDA)
Licence for coarse fish and eels for whole area on annual or one-day
basis.

Wessex Water Authority (WWA)
Licence for coarse fish and eels on an annual, weekly or daily basis.

Yorkshire Water Authority (YWA)
Licence covering all species for whole area available on an annual, weekly or daily basis. Also similar licence excluding waters north of the River Exe.

Index